QUANTUM IDENTITY ALIGNMENT™

THE FOUNDATION

A Practical Guide to Align Your Frequency & Transform Your Life

By: C. David Knox II

Table of Contents

Dedication

For every seeker who knows there is more— for those longing to
rise beyond cycles, heal old patterns,
and stand in lasting truth.

This book is dedicated to the seekers, the dreamers, the wounded,
and the rising.

May it serve as your blueprint for a permanent spiritual foundation:
anchoring you in higher consciousness, recalibrating your mind,
body, spirit.

Acknowledgements

First and foremost, I give thanks to God-consciousness—the eternal source of wisdom, guidance, and alignment that has carried me through every season of this journey. Without this divine current, none of what you hold in your hands would exist.

I acknowledge the full spectrum of life that has shaped me— the deep love and the profound loss. Both have been my teachers, forging me into who I am today in ways I could not have discovered otherwise.

I honor every experience, every person, every place, and every situation that has crossed my path, for each one carried a lesson and contributed to this becoming.

I especially honor those who endured me during the years when I was not as conscious, when I moved in lower vibrations and fought the grip of addiction. Your patience, presence, and even your absence became catalysts for growth that I will never take lightly.

To my parents, whose strength and resilience are etched into my very bloodline—thank you for showing me that anything is possible. The power and perseverance that flow through me are direct reflections of you, and I carry your legacy forward with gratitude and love.

To my mentors and teachers, both past and present, who poured into me. Each perspective shaped this work and reminded me that truth is never confined to one path.

To my children, who are my greatest teachers of patience, love, and purpose—you are the living proof that resilience creates legacy.

To the men and women I've coached, counseled, and walked alongside—you have shown me that this work is not just theory, but living transformation. Your stories breathe life into every page of this book.

And finally, to all seekers—freethinkers and conscious creators—this book is for you. You remind me that transformation is a together-journey into higher consciousness.

Preface

I chased transformation for years—books, seminars, coaching, therapy, even religion. Each gave me something: growth, wisdom, healing, spiritual breakthroughs.

But none of it brought lasting transformation. Some wounds lingered. Others resurfaced. Too often, I found myself circling the same patterns again. It was like rowing with one oar—you move, but you never get across.

"Growth was real. But it was never complete." — D. Knox

The tipping point came with my divorce. It forced me to face what trauma and addiction had already revealed: surface change was never enough. What I needed wasn't patches or pieces. I needed a complete identity shift. New thoughts. New habits. New energy. A new reality. A new alignment. A new me.

"A new alignment, a new me." — D. Knox

Let me be clear—I didn't get here by doing everything right. I got here by doing a lot of things wrong. For years, I stumbled, failed, and repeated cycles until I finally began to see what truly worked. In many ways, I became a master of mistakes. Those mistakes shaped me into who I am today.

But my story isn't just about collapse. It's also about success. I've run several million-dollar company's. I've achieved personal milestones I once thought impossible. I've mended broken family relationships, healed pieces of childhood trauma, and overcame addiction that once had me bound.

The truth is, my transformation was built in the tension of both victory and defeat, wins and wounds. That full range is what gave birth to the framework you now hold.

I didn't arrive polished, holding a method and a book. I am someone who lived through the chaos, who kept falling and getting back up, who tasted both despair and triumph—and who eventually discovered alignment.

If you've had a life full of struggles, setbacks, and ups and downs, you'll find yourself in these pages. And here's the hope: your past does not define you. You are not sealed to what you've gone through. Just as I stepped into a new identity fully aligned, so can you. The same process that pulled me out of cycles and lifted me into alignment is now in your hands.

Introduction

Forged in Fire and Victory

The Merging of Paths

In the last 16 months, I devoted myself to permanent transformation. What you're holding brings that work together— my lived experience, the spiritual studies and intensive study of quantum principles—into a practical framework. I personally have quantum leaped three times following this framework. You're holding that result now: Quantum Identity Alignment™—proven in practice, not just theory.

I was raised in a Christian household, where I first learned the rhythm of faith and devotion. Later, I studied Islam, Buddhism, metaphysics, and the universal laws of vibration, cause and effect, correspondence, and other related subjects. At first, they seemed separate. But the deeper I went, the clearer it became: they were all pointing to the same truth.

Along this journey, I was shaped by modern voices like Abraham Hicks, Dr. Joe Dispenza, Tony Robinson, Deepak Chopra, Eckhart Tolle, and A Course in Miracles. Each experience deepened my spiritual growth and expanded my philosophical understanding.

I am not here to dismantle faith but to expand it. Every path points higher. When we merge them, we don't lose meaning—we gain depth.

The Quantum Lens

What sealed the deal for me was my in-depth study of the quantum world—not just physics, but also consciousness, coherence, resonance, vibration, energy, entanglement, and alignment. Each revealed another layer of how the unseen operates, giving structure to what once felt like pure mystery.

I quickly learned that the quantum mimics the spiritual. The behavior of the smallest atoms and particles was evidence of our interconnectivity. There was actual scientific evidence that we are all connected at the atomic level. And even more startling: what we observe or pay attention to directly influences outcomes, even at the level of atoms.

We'll unpack this more in the chapters to come. But this was the lightbulb moment for me:

- What scripture described as divine law, the quantum revealed as energetic law.
- Consciousness shapes energy.
- Frequency creates reality.
- The outer world mirrors the inner one.

The spiritual and the scientific are not rivals. They are in concert. Together, they form a blueprint for transformation.

"What I share here is not borrowed—it is revealed." — D. Knox

Beyond Traditions, Into Alignment

For some, words like "quantum" or "frequency" are dismissed as New Age or unbiblical. But my journey began in the church. And the deeper I went, the more I saw: beyond religion are universal principles that God placed into creation.

Call it Jesus, Allah, Source, or Spirit—the name changes, but the truth remains: the kingdom is within.

This book unpacks those principles in a way that is practical, mechanical, and real—so you can stop circling the same loops and finally take the driver's seat of your life.

This body of work is born from my life experiences, my study of spiritual and metaphysical teachings, my exploration of the laws of the universe, and my time in religion—clarified through quantum science and strengthened by my connection with God-consciousness.

It carries frequency, and it will speak directly to you if you allow it.

This book is the beginning of a body of work that will unfold over the years. But even now, within these pages, you will find keys that merge the spiritual, the scientific, and the universal—keys that can shift your identity, your frequency, your life.

The mysteries of life are not beyond you. They can be understood. They can be lived. They can be transformed.

Most importantly, this will remind you that the power has always been within you. As scripture says: "The kingdom of God is within you."

The Framework for Everlasting Change

What emerged from my collapse was not just survival—it was a blueprint for a new life. The blueprint for what I now call Quantum Identity Alignment™.

This is not a theory. It's a framework for everlasting change, rooted in three interconnected dimensions of your being:

- ○ Mind > Your thoughts, beliefs, and self-talk.
- ○ Body > Your environment, habits, health, and physical choices.
- ○ Spirit > Your alignment with Source, faith, and higher consciousness.

When all three are aligned, transformation is permanent. And even when one area falters, the others hold you steady until you can rise again.

This is why so many attempts at self-improvement fail: they focus only on one dimension—mindset, body, or spirit—without addressing the whole. But true transformation requires the full trinity.

This is the foundation of our journey together. Page by page, you'll learn how to reprogram your mind, elevate your body and environment, and anchor yourself spiritually, so alignment becomes your new lifestyle.

This is not about partial healing. This is about full alignment.

This is not about faith alone. This is about frequency.

This is not about mystery. This is about mechanics.

"Alignment is the key that unlocks transformation." — D. Knox

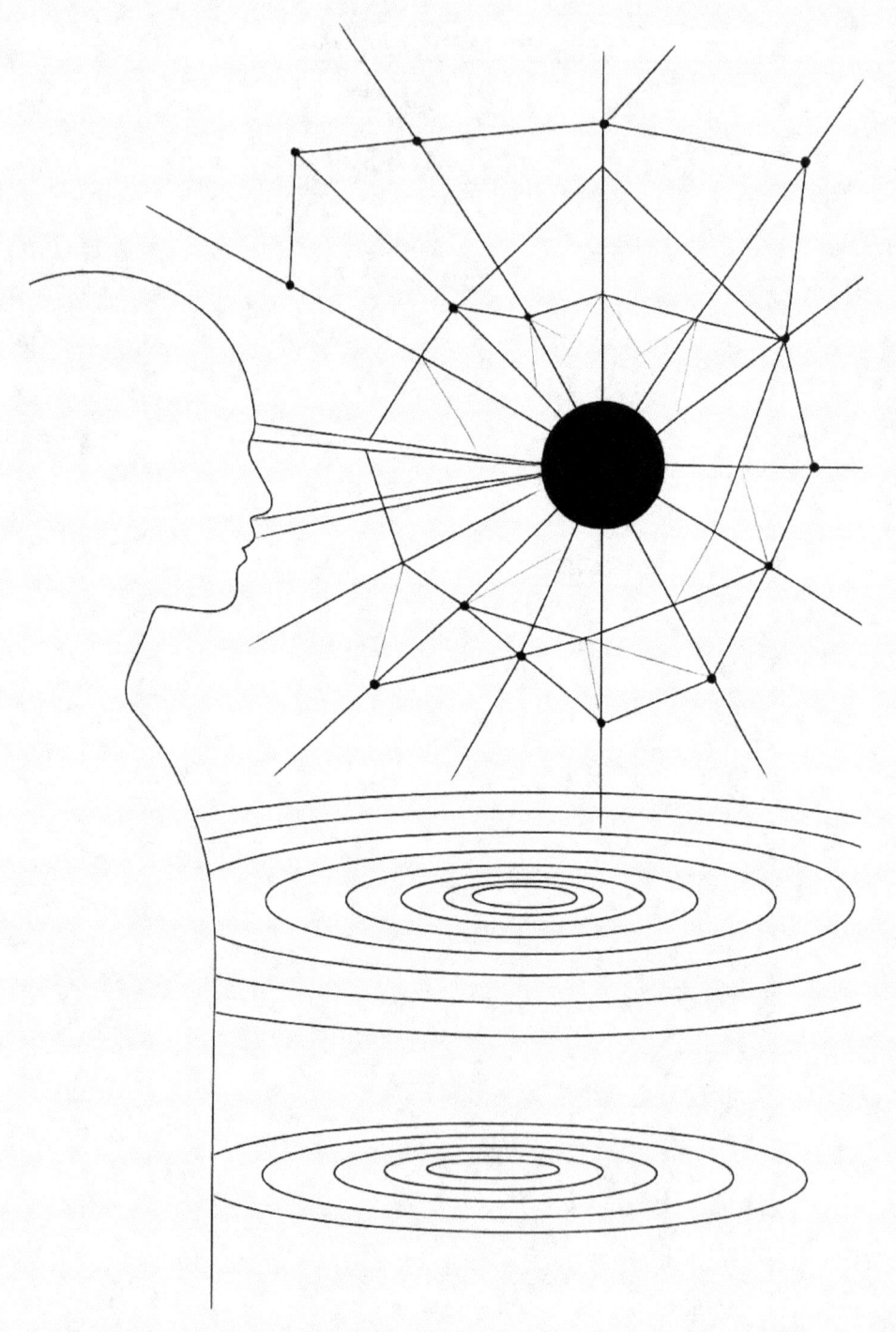

The Quantum Field: Possibility | Observation | Connection

A major part of this work is drawn from my lived experience. None of what you're about to read is theory sitting in the clouds — it's the result of practices I had to walk through, bleed through, and breathe through in real time. The techniques in this book didn't just shape my philosophy; they gave me evidence. Evidence that change is possible. Evidence that identity is not fixed. Evidence that the self can be rebuilt from the inside out.

But before any of that showed up, life collapsed around me.

Not in a dramatic, cinematic way — but in that slow, heavy, unmistakable way where everything you've been carrying suddenly asks to be faced. Several life-altering events converged at once, and for a moment, it felt like the ground I'd built myself on was dissolving beneath my feet.

Over time, though, I began to understand what both quantum science and spiritual wisdom point to: collapse is not destruction — it's reorganization. It's the crumbling of an old shell so a new frequency can emerge. It's the identity we've outgrown giving way, sometimes forcefully, to the identity we're meant to embody next.

In that season, I had to choose.

Either the pressure would break me, or it would become the friction that revealed the strongest, clearest version of myself.

Now lets step in the Quantum...

 In quantum physics, before a wave collapses into form, it exists as infinite potential. Collapse doesn't end possibility—it focuses it into one lived reality. Spirit has always taught the same. Scripture says, "Behold, I make all things new." (Revelation 21:5)

My crisis wasn't the death of me. It was the narrowing of possibilities into a new identity. It was, in truth, an invitation.

A Simple Quantum Primer

Before I take you deeper, let me pause. Throughout this book, you'll see me use words like quantum, the field, frequency, resonance, and coherence. These aren't just technical terms—they are the building blocks of how reality itself operates. To make sure we're on the same page, let's break them down in plain, practical language, with enough depth so you can begin to feel how they work together in your everyday life.

Quantum

At its simplest, quantum points to the smallest building blocks of reality—the level beneath atoms where things don't act like solid objects but like possibilities. At this level, reality is fluid, waiting for direction. Instead of being fixed and predictable, everything exists in a state of potential, like a menu of outcomes waiting to be chosen.

The Field

The field is the invisible sea of energy and information that connects everything. Imagine Wi-Fi for existence: you can't see it, but it carries signals everywhere, instantly. Your thoughts, emotions, and actions are like signals being broadcast into this field, and the field responds by mirroring them back into your lived experience.

Frequency

Frequency is the language the field listens to. Every thought, every emotion, every action you take has a measurable energetic vibration—like a song you're broadcasting into the universe. High-frequency states (gratitude, joy, clarity, love) generate expansion, ease, and synchronicity. Low-frequency states (fear, anger, shame, resentment) create contraction, delay, and struggle. The field doesn't respond to what you say you want—it responds to the frequency you are. Frequency is your true signature, the energetic "tone" that tells the field who you are becoming.

Resonance

Resonance explains why things that vibrate alike amplify each other. If you've ever seen two tuning forks—strike one and the other begins to hum in sympathy—you've seen resonance in action. Human beings do the same thing. Ever walked into a room and felt the "vibe" immediately, without anyone saying a word? That's resonance. At the quantum level, your personal frequency harmonizes with other frequencies, attracting people, experiences, and outcomes that "match your tune."

Coherence

Coherence is when your thoughts, emotions, and actions line up, creating a clean, powerful signal. Think of a choir: when everyone sings in sync, the sound is full, rich, and clear. When they're off-key, it's scattered and jarring. Your life works the same way. When your thoughts say one thing, your emotions feel another, and your actions do something else, you send a scrambled message into the field. But when all three align, your broadcast becomes unmistakable. Coherence is the state where your energy carries clarity—and clarity attracts results.

"The field doesn't respond to what you want. It mirrors who you are." — D. Knox

The Double-Slit Experiment: Waves of Possibility

Imagine this: scientists fire tiny particles—electrons—at a barrier with two narrow slits cut into it. Behind the barrier is a screen that records where the particles land.

Logically, you'd expect them to act like little marbles. Two slits, two neat clusters on the screen. One slit, one pile. Two slits, two piles. End of story.

But that's not what happened.

Instead, the electrons created an interference pattern—ripples of light and dark bands across the screen, like waves of water colliding. The electrons weren't behaving like particles at all. They were behaving like waves.

And here's the astonishing part: each electron didn't go through one slit or the other—it appeared to go through both slits at once. It existed as a cloud of pure possibility, spread across space, holding

every potential path simultaneously.

In other words, until something forced the choice, the electron remained undefined. Infinite.

Then came the twist that shook science to its core.

When researchers placed a detector at the slits to observe which path the electron took, the wave of possibilities collapsed instantly. No more interference pattern. No more wave. The electron suddenly chose one slit or the other.

The act of observation itself changed the outcome.

Let that settle in: the electron behaved differently simply because it was being watched.

> Observation isn't passive—it's creative. What you focus on collapses into your reality." — D. Knox

Why This Matters

At the smallest level of existence, life doesn't behave as fixed matter. It behaves as a possibility.

Every moment is like that cloud of electrons—holding countless futures. What you observe, expect, and focus on determines which path collapses into form.

Science calls it quantum mechanics.

Scripture calls it faith.

Mystics call it manifestation.

Different words. Same truth.

"As a man thinketh in his heart, so is he." (Proverbs 23:7)

"According to your faith be it unto you." (Matthew 9:29)

"What you focus on expands." — A Course in Miracles

Enter Einstein: "Spooky Action at a Distance"

The mysteries didn't stop there. Scientists later discovered that once particles interact, they remain mysteriously connected—even when separated by miles or light-years. Shift one, and the other shifts instantly. Einstein, though skeptical, couldn't deny it. He called it "spooky action at a distance."

What unsettled him is now confirmation for us: at the deepest level, everything is connected.

This is why collective prayer moves energy across nations. Why trauma echoes through family lines. Why one person's gratitude can lift an entire room. Entanglement isn't just physics—it's how love, presence, and energy ripple across humanity.

"Your consciousness is not isolated. Every shift you make resonates across the whole." — D. Knox

Life as the Lab

Think about your own life as a living double-slit experiment When you constantly observe lack ("I'll never get ahead," "There are no good people left to love"), you collapse your reality into lack.

When you constantly observe possibility ("The universe is conspiring for me," "Love is available," "I am expanding"), you collapse your reality into abundance.

Two people can face the same crisis—a job loss, a breakup, a diagnosis—and experience entirely different outcomes. One sees disaster. The other sees opportunity. Same slits. Same electrons.

Different observations. Different lives.

Your attention is sacred currency. The stories you replay, the emotions you feed, the thoughts you empower—these are the detectors collapsing your potential into form.

Case Study: Shifting the Lens

One of my clients, Sarah, came to me after being laid off from a company she'd worked at for 15 years. To her, the layoff was devastating. She observed betrayal, lack of security, and loss of identity. Her attention collapsed her reality into despair. Every conversation circled around what she had lost. Every action broadcasts fear. And the opportunities she tried to pursue seemed to evaporate.

We began working on observation—shifting her lens. She started small: journaling her gratitude, declaring, "The field is reorganizing for my good," and practicing meditation. She stopped replaying the narrative of loss and started observing possibilities. We employed high-frequency techniques and did more work. Within two months, Sarah was offered a position with a smaller firm that provided her with the flexibility and creative freedom she hadn't experienced in years. Her observation shifted—and her reality followed.

Staying Open to Possibility

Observation is a double-edged sword.

- ○ Focus on fear, and it collapses into your life.
- ○ Focus on gratitude, and joy multiplies.
- ○ Focus on abundance, and doors open where walls once stood.

The danger is in narrowing your lens too tightly. When you decide, "This is the only way my life can go," you collapse infinite possibilities into one narrow path.

Nature reminds us to stay open. A caterpillar doesn't fight the cocoon—it surrenders to transformation. Winter doesn't mean death—it makes way for spring.

Don't assume rejection means unworthiness. Don't assume collapse means punishment. Don't assume a closed door means the end.

Stay open, and the universe has room to surprise you.

"Your possibilities are waves. Stay open, and the field will meet you with more than you imagined." — D. Knox

Key Takeaways

- The Double-Slit Experiment demonstrates that reality exists as possibilities until it is observed.

- Observation collapses waves into form—your focus is not passive, it's creative.

- Einstein's "spooky action at a distance" demonstrates that everything is interconnected—your shifts ripple outward.

- Life is your lab. Crisis isn't just loss—it's a chance to collapse a higher reality into form.

- Stay open. Don't collapse into limitation. Stay in resonance with possibility.

"Crisis isn't the end. It's the portal into your next identity." — D. Knox

Crisis Was My Invitation

When my life began to fall apart, it felt like annihilation. My marriage and family unraveled. My business and financial stability collapsed. The roles I thought defined me—husband, father, provider, man of certainty—shattered overnight.

I remember lying awake at three in the morning, staring at the ceiling, my chest tight, my thoughts circling like vultures.

Why me? Why now? What did I do wrong?

The silence that followed was brutal. At the time, I thought it was punishment. Maybe God had turned His face from me. Maybe life had finally cashed the debt of my mistakes. What I had built turned to dust, and I was left with nothing but the ache of emptiness.

But here's the truth I now know: crisis wasn't punishment. It was an invitation.

Collapse in Quantum and Spirit

In quantum physics, collapse isn't destruction—it's reorganization.

Before a wave collapses into form, it exists as infinite potential.

Collapse isn't the death of possibility; it's the narrowing into one reality.

Looking back, that's exactly what happened to me. The collapse of my family, my business, my identity—it wasn't random. It was the collapse of an old waveform that could no longer sustain who I was meant to become.

Mystics and scientists agree on this point: breakdown is a form of reordering. Crisis cracks the shell, allowing a higher frequency to emerge.

 "Behold, I make all things new." — Revelation 21:5

The Quantum Lens of Collapse

Science and spirit speak the same language here.

Quantum physics refers to it as wave collapse—a field of infinite potential that narrows into a single form.

Mystics call it death and rebirth—the falling away of the old so the new can emerge.

And life itself calls it a crisis—the moment when what you thought you needed is stripped away, so what you actually need can arrive.

 "Indeed, with hardship comes ease." — Qur'an 94:6

"Unless a grain of wheat falls into the earth and dies, it remains alone; but if it dies, it bears much fruit." — John 12:24

Collapse wasn't the end of me. It was the soil of my becoming.

Nature's Reminder

The universe speaks through patterns. Look at nature and you'll see it everywhere:

- A caterpillar collapses into a cocoon of stillness before it can emerge as a butterfly.
- A forest fire ravages the land, yet enriches the soil for new growth.
- Winter strips the trees bare, but spring follows with renewal.

Every collapse in nature holds the same truth: destruction makes room for rebirth.

My crisis was no different.

And if you are in a season of collapse right now, hear me clearly: this is not the end. This is the soil of your becoming.

> "Crisis isn't the end. It's the portal into your next identity." — D. Knox

The Three-Pronged Approach: Mind- Body- Spirit

Out of that collapse came the blueprint for what I now call Quantum Identity Alignment™—the framework for everlasting change through the alignment of mind, body, and spirit.

This is the foundation of everything you're about to learn in this book. Lasting transformation doesn't happen by changing just one part of you—it only holds when all three dimensions shift together.

- o If you change your thoughts but not your body or environment, your biology and surroundings will still pull you back.

- o If you change your routines but not your spirit, you run out of fuel when life tests you.

- o If you ignite your spirit but neglect your body and mind, the fire burns out before it can anchor.

That's why Quantum Identity Alignment™ isn't a quick fix or a band-aid. It is a full-life recalibration that rewires your identity on all three levels at once. Together, mind, body, and spirit form the tripod of transformation. Remove one leg, and the structure wobbles.

Strengthen all three, and you build permanent alignment.

And here's the grace in it: even when one leg weakens—when your body is tired, your spirit feels heavy, or your mind is clouded—the other two can hold you steady until you rise again.

I want to pause here and be transparent. I didn't come to this understanding as a guru on a mountaintop. I came to it as a man in ashes.

I became, in many ways, a master of mistakes. Failed attempts at rebuilding. Nights numbing myself instead of healing. Days performing strength when inside, I was unraveling.

And yet, every mistake became a teacher. Every collapse contained wisdom. Every failure revealed a doorway.

That's why I can speak to you now, not from theory but from the trenches. What you'll read in these chapters isn't distant philosophy—it's life... living for 52 years in its fullness and using the techniques in this book to transform my life and Quantum Leap into my new identity.

As you move through this book, you'll notice each chapter touches one of these three dimensions (mind ~ body ~ spirit). Sometimes we'll focus on rewiring the mind. Other times, on healing the body (which includes both your physical health and the environment you live in). And other times, we'll deal with the spirit.

But always, they weave together, because alignment is not one-dimensional—it is whole.

"Every step, every sip, every breath is a frequency broadcast. Choose the self you are becoming." — D. Knox

Key Takeaways

- Crisis isn't punishment—it's an invitation to evolve.
- Collapse is divine reorganization, shaping a higher version of you.
- Nature shows that destruction always precedes rebirth.
- True transformation anchors through mind, body, and spirit working in harmony.
- Failure and breakdown are the soil of becoming.
- Every breath, thought, and choice broadcasts your next identity.

In the next chapter, we'll step into the field itself—where possibility is infinite, and observation collapses into reality. That's where your new identity begins.

OLD
IDENTITY

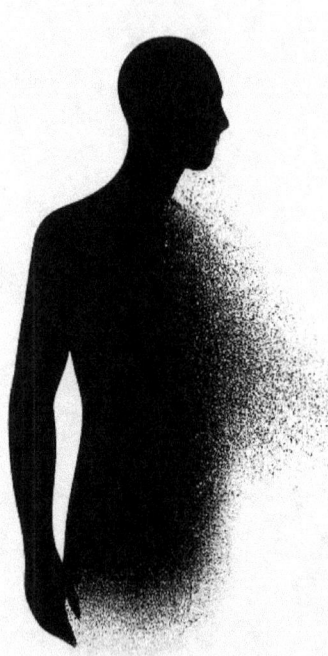

NEW
IDENTITY

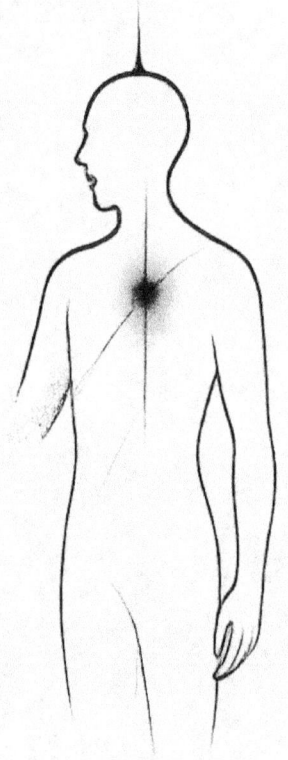

Identity Mapping: The Old Self vs. The New Self

When I first began this journey, I realized something sobering: no matter how many affirmations I spoke or how many prayers I offered, I was still operating from the same identity. Fear, guilt, and anger were the engines behind my choices.

If I wanted to rise to a higher frequency, I couldn't just think new thoughts. I had to become a new self.

That was my first real breakthrough. I stopped asking, "How do I fix my circumstances?" and instead asked:

"Who am I being right now—and who am I choosing to become?"

This shift is the foundation of Quantum Identity Alignment™. Because until you see the identity you're living from today, you cannot step into the one you're called to embody tomorrow.

Why Identity Matters

At the quantum level, reality is fluid. It exists as waves of possibility until something collapses into form. That collapse doesn't happen randomly—it's shaped by consciousness.

Dr. Joe Dispenza puts it simply: "Your personality creates your personal reality." The way you think, feel, and act forms the electromagnetic broadcast of your identity—and the field mirrors it back as your life.

That's why people repeat the same loops: new jobs, same stress. New partners, same heartbreak. New year, same disappointments. The field doesn't respond to what you wish for. It responds to the identity you live from.

Scripture echoes this truth:

"As a man thinketh in his heart, so is he." (Proverbs 23:7)

"Indeed, Allah will not change the condition of a people until they change what is in themselves." (Qur'an 13:11)

The shift begins with identity. When you map out your Old Identity and step into your New Identity, you collapse a new possibility into form.

What Is a Quantum Leap?

A quantum leap isn't slow, incremental change. It's an identity shift. It's moving from one state of being to another so completely that your old self cannot recognize the life you're living now.

That doesn't mean skipping the process. It means creating

clarity: Who am I right now? Who am I becoming? And then aligning every thought, feeling, and action with that future self until the leap is undeniable.

This is where the Identity Mapping Exercise becomes your blueprint.

The Identity Mapping Exercise

This is where your transformation begins. If you don't know the self you're leaving behind and the self you're stepping into, you'll keep circling. This exercise is your roadmap for a quantum leap.

Take out your journal. Draw two large circles or two columns side by side. Label one:

Old Identity (Who I Am Now)

New Identity (Who I Am Becoming)

1. Old Identity: Who I Am Now

This is the self that has carried you here. It may not be "bad," but it's incomplete. Below are some prompts you can use to touch on areas of your life that need transformation as you current self. You are not limited to these prompts if there is something that resonates with you identify it.

- What is your current operating base? Example: people pleaser, guilt, shame, etc
- Beliefs: The thoughts you keep rehearsing about life, money, love, or yourself.
  (Ex: "I'm always behind." "I'm not worthy of real love." "Money slips through my hands.")
- Habits: The routines and behaviors you live with daily.

(Ex: procrastinating, overworking, numbing with food, avoiding conflict.)

- Characteristics: The traits you identify with right now.
  (Ex: "people pleaser," "always the strong one," "the fixer," "unreliable.")

- Body / Health: How your physical body currently feels and functions.
  (Ex: carrying extra weight, feeling tired, tension in the chest, shallow breathing.

- Havingness / Finances: Your current relationship with money, success, and abundance.
  (Ex: "never enough," "just scraping by," "hustle mode," or even "earning well but always stressed.")

- Relationships: The patterns you repeat with others.
  (Ex: attracting unavailable partners, overgiving to friends, staying in toxic ties.)

- Family Dynamics: What roles do you play in your family?
  (Ex: the peacekeeper, the black sheep, the provider, the one who sacrifices their dreams.)

- Key Loops: The phrases that echo in your mind.
  (Ex: "I always mess this up." "I can't trust anyone." "I'll never get ahead.")

- Don't sugarcoat it. Don't hold back. This is your honest mirror.

2. New Identity: Who I Am Becoming

Now, across from every Old Identity entry, script the aligned version of yourself. This is the next version of yourself you aspire to become. This is new frequency you're choosing to broadcast. Write it in the present tense, as though it already exists.

- ○ Beliefs: "I am in rhythm with my life." "I am worthy of love and respect." "I am a magnet for financial flow."
- ○ Habits: "I prioritize what matters most." "I finish what I start." "I move my body daily."
- ○ Characteristics: "I set boundaries with ease." "I am disciplined and creative." "I lead from peace, not pressure."
- ○ Body / Health: "I am strong, energized, and clear." "My body is aligned with vitality."
- ○ Havingness / Finances: "I live in a universe of supply." "I attract money and manage it wisely."
- ○ Relationships: "I attract healthy, reciprocal love." "I give without overextending."
- ○ Family Dynamics: "I honor my family, but I no longer carry their expectations as my own."

Practical Tips for Mapping

Be thorough and take a deep dive, fill the page. Expose the full story of your Old Identity so you can release it.

Write honestly. Even if it stings, capture the exact phrases or feelings that have been looping in your head.

Make the New Identity believable. Don't jump to "I'm a billionaire living on the beach." Stretch yourself, but stay in resonance with what feels possible. The field responds to coherence, not fantasy

New Identity Statement: Let this statement include mind, body and spirit.

Example: I am living healthy taking care of my body. I am no longer operating out of guilt and lack. I move with confidence and alignment with my higher self claiming all the blessings and abundance that is rightfully mine. I am honoring myself and what resonates with me in all my decisions and actions.

Completing Identity Mapping (Forward-Identity Method)

You've mapped your Old Identity and defined your New Identity. From here, we shift from analysis to embodiment. We honor the past, but we don't relive it. Those experiences carried you this far; now they no longer define you. Our work is to install the new identity—thoughts, words, actions, and energy—so your nervous system, habits, and choices align with who you're becoming. The chapters that follow will install a foundation for your new Identity so this change is permeant.

Traditional approaches often keep you looping on old stories. This method is different: we stabilize resonance with your new identity now. You'll practice feeling its frequency, speaking its language, and moving as that person in real situations. When moments arise that used to trigger the old self, you'll ask:

"How would my New Self respond?"

Then you respond that way—consistently. That's the leap.

Daily Identity Installation: Mantra + Practice

The Mantra (read aloud—customize the brackets)

I am no longer a prisoner of my past conditions or traumas.

I release what no longer serves me and step forward as my New Self: [New Identity Name/Title].

My thoughts, words, and actions align with [3 core traits—e.g., clarity, courage, compassion].

Today, I move in [key behaviors—e.g., honest boundaries, focused work, steady breath].

I choose [one anchor value—e.g., truth] over [old pattern—e.g., people-pleasing].

I embody [desired feeling—e.g., calm authority] in every room I enter.

I am this now. And I remain in alignment as I move through my day.

Optional Power Phrase

"I stabilize my new identity with every choice I make today."

A. *Morning Protocol*

Recall the New Identity (60 sec)

Read your New Identity statement: "I am ___

Physiology first (60 sec)

Three slow breaths; lengthen the exhale. Sit/stand tall—let the body model the new identity.

Feel the Frequency (60–90 sec)

Evoke the emotion/essence of your New Self (e.g., calm authority, joyful certainty). Let it spread through chest, face, posture.

Speak the Mantra (60–90 sec)

Say it out loud, steady and clear (see below). Repeat 2–3 times.

Micro-Rehearsals (60–90 sec)

Mentally rehearse 2–3 likely moments today where the old self might appear. See your New Self's response—voice, words, body language, next action.

Implementation Intention Action Plan

"If (old trigger) happens, I will pause (New Self action/phrase)

State shift: "Breath long, shoulders soft—I lead with [trait]."

Choice line: "I don't negotiate with my old patterns. I choose [new action] now."

B. Evening Lock-In (2 minutes)

3 Wins as New Self (what you did, said, or chose in alignment)

1 Tighten (tomorrow's adjustment—one sentence)

Gratitude (for the day you created as the New Self)

Reminders:

Keep it simple. Same mantra daily for at least 21 days; tweak only the bracketed fields as needed.

Name the Identity. A short title (e.g., "Calm, Decisive Creator") gives your mind a handle to grab in real time.

Feel > words. The emotional tone you generate while speaking the mantra is the glue; let your body match it.

Decide at the fork. Each trigger is a doorway—step through as the New Self, even in tiny ways. Tiny choices compound.

This is the essence of the quantum leap: not rehashing the past, but embodying the future self—now—and confirming it with your choices until it becomes your baseline.

Case Study: Lisa's Quantum Leap

Old Identity:

Lisa was cycling old loops—frustration, stalled progress, and alcohol as a coping pattern—keeping her anchored to guilt and self-doubt.

How she shifted (using QIA tools): Through Identity Mapping (old vs. chosen self) and following the steps outlined in the book combined with One-on-One couching she installed a new internal stance and foundation to start her Quantum Leap

New Identity (lived reality):

"I am a clear, sovereign woman. I live alcohol-free, keep my word to myself, and move at the pace of alignment."

Outcome: Within two weeks, Lisa made a decisive quantum leap—her behavior matched her new identity. As of this manuscript, she is two months alcohol-free, living a focused life, cleaner decisions, and forward momentum on personal goals. This transformation is a direct result of doing the work—following the steps, and choosing the new identity daily.

None of this works unless you do the work. Identity shifts when action agrees with truth. — D. Knox

Key Takeaways

- Identity is the framework of reality.

- Old Identity is programming. New Identity is a possibility.

- Mapping your beliefs, habits, body, relationships, and loops reveals the gap.

- Writing your New Identity in detail collapses new probabilities into form

- Quantum leaping is not fantasy—it is clarity + embodiment + alignment.

The Body as the First Battlefield

When transformation began for me, my mind was in chaos. I was flooded with loops of despair—betrayal, resentment, sadness. Nights without sleep left me hollow. Anxiety gripped my chest. My nervous system was wrecked.

I thought: How do I fix this? Where do I even start? And then it hit me: I couldn't think my way out. My mind was too full of static. But I could move my body. That was simple, physical, third-dimensional. Something I could control, so I started there.

"Movement was my first medicine." — D. Knox

Movement as Medicine

I began walking and running in the mornings. No master plan, no strict program—just motion. It became a doorway, a release valve for the pressure inside. Sweat wasn't just burning calories—it was burning off pain.

Trauma doesn't just live in the mind. Neuroscience confirms what mystics long taught: trauma lodges in the body. It hides in your muscles, your breath, your tissues.

Every drop of sweat felt like grief leaving me. Each step was a declaration: I am still here.

I even set a goal to lose 5–10 pounds—not only to change the mirror, but to shed spiritual weight. And it worked. Shedding pounds became identity work. Because when you see a new version of yourself in the mirror, you start believing in that version internally too.

Sometimes after running, I'd sit in the sauna or steam room. The heat felt like detox. Toxins left my pores. Old energy burned off. Each session felt like resurrection.

That's why I tell people: exercise isn't just fitness. It's frequency work.

- ○ Movement transmutes energy.
- ○ Sweat is grief leaving.
- ○ Weight loss can be spiritual shedding.

Walking Into Alignment

My first step wasn't into a gym. It was into nature. Morning after morning, I walked outside—feet on the earth, lungs filling with fresh air, body syncing with the rhythm of creation. Simple, but sacred.

And then something unexpected happened: I attracted a walking partner.

She had a prior experience very similar to mine. For nearly six months, we walked together for miles. We laughed, processed, and reflected. She became, in many ways, an angel sent to walk me through my season.

That's the beauty of alignment: when you shift your frequency, the universe responds with support.

Movement released what my mind couldn't. Nature grounded me. Companionship lifted me. Together, it rewired my mornings into a ritual and reset my nervous system into coherence.

Water: Life's Original Frequency

The next step was water. Not casually. Not six glasses here and there. I committed to a gallon a day.

The body is 60% water. The brain? Nearly 80%. Even your bones hold water. That means every cell, every tissue, every thought is swimming in a liquid field.

And water is not neutral. Dr. Masaru Emoto's experiments showed that water responds to vibration, words, and intention. Bless water with gratitude, and its molecular structure shifts into beauty.

When you drink water, you're not just hydrating; you're also replenishing your body's essential fluids. You're programming your frequency.

I began drinking consciously. Each sip was an affirmation: I am cleansing. I am renewing. I am recharging.

> "Water is not just hydration. It is programming for your frequency." — D. Knox

Then came food. Frequency you can taste

I noticed how living foods—fruits, vegetables, greens still buzzing with sunlight—lifted me. My energy was lighter, my mind was calmer, and my emotions were more balanced.

But processed foods did the opposite. They weighed me down, left me foggy, pulled me into stagnation. This wasn't just nutrition—it was physics.

Food carries frequency. Every bite is either anchoring you to your old self or fueling your new one.

- ○ Living foods = high vibration, coherence, clarity.
- ○ Dead foods = stagnation, density, decay

> "Food is frequency. Living foods fuel life. Dead foods fuel decay." — D. Knox

Identity Alignment Practice: Begin in the Body

If you're in crisis, don't try to think your way out. Start with the body.

- ○ Move: Walk, run, stretch, sweat. Let movement transmute the energy your mind cannot.
- ○ Hydrate: One gallon a day. Bless it. Drink it consciously. Water is a life force.
- ○ Eat Alive: Living foods elevate your vibration. Processed foods tether you to the old self.
- ○ Breathe: Deep breathing tells your nervous system that you are safe. Safety creates space for a new identity.

Each act is a broadcast. A signal to the field. A declaration of who you are becoming.

Key Takeaways

- The body is the first battlefield of transformation. Trauma lives in your tissues, not just your thoughts.

- Movement is medicine. Sweat is grief leaving.

- Water carries memory—drinking with intention reprograms your frequency.

- Food is frequency. Living foods elevate, processed foods stagnate.

- Each physical choice is a signal to the field about who you are becoming.

"Every step, every sip, every bite is a frequency broadcast. Choose the self you are becoming." — D. Knox

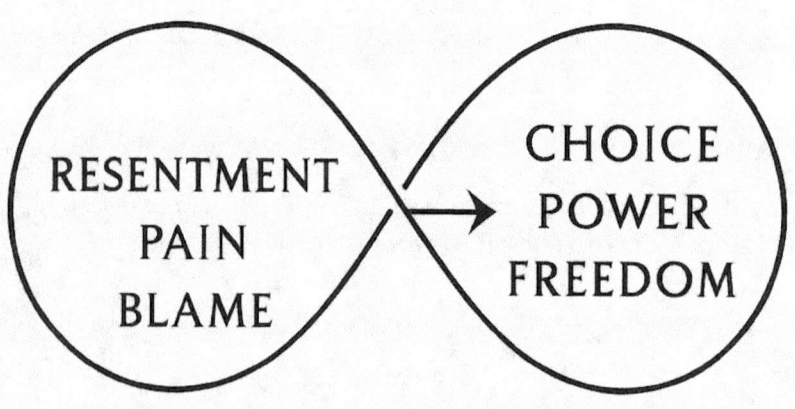

Breaking the Blame Loop: Firing My Inner Victim

As days stretched into weeks, I realized something deeper: the true loss wasn't just my wife, my family, or my business—it was me. I had lost my sense of who I was.

Resentment became my daily oxygen. Each morning, I replayed the same reel: the fights, the betrayals, the collapse. My mind was like Netflix stuck on autoplay, and every episode ended the same way—with me as the victim.

I told myself I was "processing." The truth? I wasn't processing—I was programming.

Programming the Victim Identity

Neuroscience shows that every time you recall a memory, you don't just replay it—you re-record it. This is called memory reconsolidation. The more I rehearsed betrayal, the deeper the grooves in my brain became. Psychology calls this rumination. Spirit calls it bondage.

Quantum physics calls it collapse. The observer effect teaches us that what you focus on, you collapse into reality. And in my case, the only possibility I kept collapsing was the identity of the victim.

The field wasn't responding to fairness or tears—it was responding to my vibration.

> "Life doesn't give you what you want. It gives you what you vibrate." — D. Knox

Scripture confirms the same:

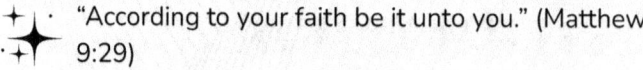 "According to your faith be it unto you." (Matthew 9:29)

"Indeed, Allah will not change the condition of a people until they change what is in themselves." (Qur'an 13:11)

Science and spirit agree: reality mirrors resonance.

The Seduction of Blame

Blame is seductive because it feels like power. You get to be right; someone else gets to be wrong. But that righteousness is a mirage.

Psychology refers to this as secondary gain—the hidden payoff we receive from staying stuck. For me, blame gave temporary relief from responsibility. But in the long run, it imprisoned me.

It also had a biological hook. Every time I replayed my story, my body released cortisol and adrenaline. My nervous system became addicted to the very emotions I despised.

Eckhart Tolle refers to this as the pain-body—an emotional entity that feeds on the past and grows stronger every time it is reawakened.

> "If you broadcast victimhood, life will hand you more proof that you're a victim." — D. Knox

The Silent Perpetuator: Retelling the Story

Here's the hardest truth I faced: every time I told my story, I wasn't releasing pain—I was reinforcing it. What felt like therapy was actually programming.

Neuroscience calls this reconsolidation. Spirit calls it an agreement. Every retelling was a frequency broadcast into the field.

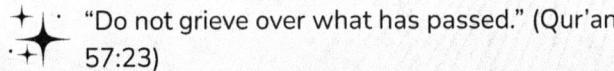 "Do not grieve over what has passed." (Qur'an 57:23)

Rumi wrote: "Try not to resist the changes that come your way... How do you know the side you are used to is better than the one to come?"

But I wasn't listening. Each retelling was pressing refresh on victimhood.

> "Every retelling is a reprogramming. Stop broadcasting the old story." — D. Knox

The Turning Point: From "Why Me?" to "For Me"

The loop finally cracked the day I asked a new question:

"What if this isn't happening to me—what if it's happening for me?"

That shift changed everything. Pain became a portal. Collapse became initiation.

At the moment, I couldn't see it. Ten years of marriage and business had dissolved—it felt catastrophic. The only thing I could cling to was faith. Faith whispered: There is a higher intelligence guiding your life, even if you can't yet see it.

Years later, hindsight is clear:

- I was being freed from self-destructive loops.
- I was being shown hidden parts of myself I never would have faced otherwise.
- I was being prepared for a higher purpose.

Deepak Chopra said, "In the process of letting go, you will lose many things from the past, but you will find yourself."

That's exactly what happened.
And this principle is not just mine—it's universal.

- Lose a job? It's not the end—it's redirection.
- A business deal falls apart? It wasn't in resonance with who you're becoming.
- A friendship fades? That vacuum creates space for an aligned community.

The key is to look beyond the surface. Ask: "What higher possibility is this guiding me toward?"

Hold your vibration high. Stay tuned to gratitude, not resentment; expansion, not collapse. That's how the field responds with new people, opportunities, and outcomes that match your frequency.

"What feels like the end is often an initiation into your
true beginning." — D. Knox

The Alchemy of Emotion

Here's what I learned: emotions are not enemies. Anger, grief,
fear—they are energy. And energy cannot be destroyed, only
transformed.

Abraham Hicks describes this as the emotional guidance scale:
you don't leap from despair to joy in one jump. You climb one at
a time. Anger can be the spark of courage. Grief can soften into
compassion. Fear can point you toward growth.

The Course in Miracles reminds us: "Nothing real can be
threatened. Nothing unreal exists. Herein lies the peace of God."

When you reframe pain, the very energy that enslaved you
becomes fuel for your becoming.

"Emotions are energy. You don't erase them—you
alchemize them." — D. Knox

Daily Energy Shifts

I began small, practicing shifts that built momentum:

o "Why did this happen to me?" > "This is happening for me."

o "I lost everything." > "I am creating a new reality."

o "I'm broken." > "I am rebuilding."

○ "I'm always behind." > "I am on time for my own life."

It works for the big things (divorce, business collapse) and the small (traffic, conflict, a missed opportunity). The principle is the same: you shift the energy by shifting the story.

Each reframe is a vote for your future self. Over time, those votes add up to transformation.

Key Takeaways

○ Blame feels like power, but it enslaves you.

○ Retelling the story can actually reinforce pain instead of helping to heal it.

○ Faith reframes collapse as redirection.

○ Emotions are raw energy—waiting for alchemy.

○ Small daily reframes rewire loops and build momentum.

"The loop ends the moment you choose a new frequency."
— D. Knox

Thought Detox: Reprogramming Your Inner Language

Breaking the blame loop freed me from living in the past. But once the noise of blame was silenced, I discovered something even more dangerous: the loudest critic in my life wasn't my ex, my family, or even my failures.

It was me.

The voice inside my head whispered:

"You'll never get this right."

"You're not good at keeping relationships."

"You're missing something."

"It's too late to start over. You're in the latter stages of your life, and the weight of that is too heavy."

If someone else had spoken those words to me, I would have cut them out of my life. But because it was my own inner dialogue, I tolerated it. Worse—I believed it.

> "Your self-talk is not background noise. It's the script of your reality." — D. Knox

The Quantum Power of Words

Words are not commentary; they are creation.

On the surface, words are sound waves. But on the quantum level, they are frequencies collapsing possibilities into form.

Dr. Masaru Emoto's water experiments made this clear: water crystals exposed to words like "love" and "gratitude" formed intricate, beautiful patterns, while those exposed to words like "hate" or "stupidity" fractured into chaos.

If your body is 70% water, then every phrase you whisper to yourself is shaping your biology and your reality in real time.

Psychology also supports this notion: Cognitive Behavioral Therapy (CBT) suggests that thoughts generate feelings, which in turn influence actions. Over time, words become identity.

Scripture affirms this truth:

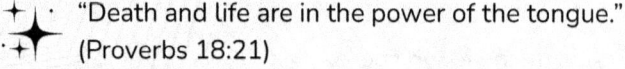 "Death and life are in the power of the tongue."
(Proverbs 18:21)

"Do not speak of that which you do not know."
(Qur'an 17:36)

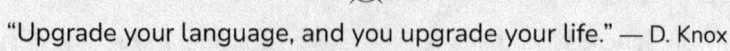
"Upgrade your language, and you upgrade your life." — D. Knox

Observer Mode: Hearing Yourself for the First Time

Psychologists estimate we think 60,000–70,000 thoughts per day. Over 80% are negative, and nearly 90% are recycled from yesterday. Unless you intervene, today is just yesterday on repeat.

When I began practicing Observer Mode, I was shocked. The loudest themes weren't visionary—they were stale reruns filled with the heaviness of regret and aging:

"You've wasted too much time."

"You'll never recover from this."

"You're too far behind to catch up."

"You're too old to start again."

Those thoughts weren't truth. They were programming. But because they carried the weight of time, they felt final. That's the danger: when we believe the clock has run out, we unconsciously stop playing the game.

My breakthrough came when I caught those whispers and asked: "Is this truth, or is this trauma talking?" Then I asked the more powerful question: "What do I want to create now?"

That single shift moved me from victim to creator.

> "Awareness breaks the loop. Observation is liberation." — D. Knox

Thought Mechanics: How Thoughts Become Things

Every thought is electromagnetic:

- ○ Electrical: Neurons fire, wiring new circuits in the brain.
- ○ Magnetic: Emotions radiate through the body.

○   Vibrational: Together, they broadcast into the field.

Replay toxic thoughts like "It's too late" or "I'll never get it right" and you collapse possibility into limitation. Upgrade your inner language, and you collapse new timelines into form.

Dr. Joe Dispenza says it plainly: "Your personality creates your personal reality."

"Language is not description. It is creation." — D. Knox

Stop–Swap–Speak: The Language Upgrade Tool

Here's the method I used to rewire my inner dialogue:

Stop > Interrupt the thought mid-loop. Catch it before it spirals.

(Ex: "It's too late for me.")

Swap > Replace it with a higher-frequency truth. Question it first: Is this truth, or is this fear of time?

(Ex: "I am right on time for my own journey

Speak > Declare it aloud. Write it down. Anchor it with an aligned action.

> "Every word you speak is a frequency collapsing into form." — D. Knox

Daily Language Upgrades

- "It's too late for me." > "I am right on time for my life."
- "I'm too old to start over." > "My wisdom gives me an advantage in creating new beginnings.
- "I'm not good at relationships." > "I am learning to love and be loved in healthy, aligned ways."
- "I've missed my chance." > "The field always offers new chances—I align with them now."

The Evening Inner Voice Ritual

One of the most powerful practices I discovered was my Evening Inner Voice Ritual. Every night before bed, I would:

1. Write down 2–3 negative phrases I caught during the day.
2. Rewrite them into higher-frequency truths.
3. Speak them aloud as I drifted into sleep.

Why before bed? As the brain shifts into alpha and theta states, the subconscious is most receptive to suggestion. The last words you feed it don't just end the day—they script the next one.

> "The voice you fall asleep to becomes the architect of tomorrow." — D. Knox

Case Study: Maria

I had a client named Maria whose most common phrase was: "I'm always behind."

That one line defined her life. She lived in constant anxiety and panic, rushing through her days as if the clock was always against her.

So I introduced her to the Stop–Swap–Speak technique.

o Stop: She caught herself in the loop of "I'm always behind."

o Swap: She replaced it with simple, believable phrases:

"I can be organized."

"I have more control over my day."

"Time is on my side."

"I am working toward balance."

o Speak: She began saying them aloud and writing them down.

But I emphasized something crucial: start small. When you're overwhelmed, the last thing you need is another giant task.

Along with the Stop Swap & Speak tool I told her to get a calendar/planner to organize her day and start waking up 20 min . earlier.

That's it.

Those two simple shifts completely changed her frequency. They pulled her off the channel of anxiety and put her on the channel of organization.

Once on that channel, she noticed the universe meeting her halfway. Ideas flowed. Inspiration replaced panic. Her family began helping more. She started saying no instead of yes to everything.

What began as two tiny actions became a ripple effect of alignment.

Maria's story proves this: it doesn't matter your age, your stage of life, or your circumstances. Transformation doesn't start with massive leaps. It starts with small upgrades in words and actions.

> "Every small upgrade shifts the channel—and once you're tuned in, the universe can play its part." — D. Knox

Coaching Lens

If you were in session with me right now, I would ask you:

- What three phrases do you repeat most often?
- Do any of them carry the weight of time—like "too late" or "I missed my chance"?
- Where did these phrases come from—family, culture, trauma?
- How can you rewrite them in alignment with your future self?
- Will you commit to rehearsing them nightly until they feel natural and comfortable?

Because here's the truth: your words are not commentary. They are commands.

Key Takeaways

- Words shape both biology and reality.
- Most thoughts are recycled programming—often tied to fear of time or failure.
- Observer Mode lets you hear and break the loop.
- Stop–Swap–Speak rewires self-talk into alignment.

○ Evening rituals reprogram your subconscious identity.

○ Small, practical upgrades (like Maria's calendar and morning routine) shift your channel—and the field responds.

"Your inner language is not background noise—it is the code of your becoming." — D. Knox

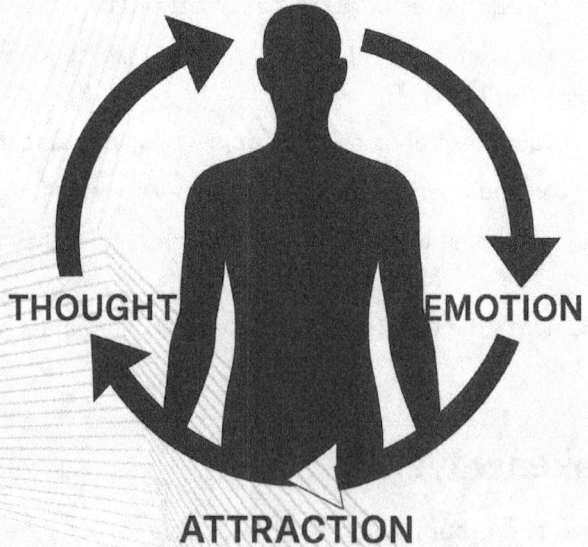

THOUGHT-EMOTION-ATTRACTION LOOP

THOUGHT

EMOTION

ATTRACTION

Emotional Frequency Calibration: Raising Your Vibrational Home

Have you ever met someone who lights up a room the moment they walk in? They don't even have to say a word—you just feel their energy. Their presence is magnetic.

And then there's the opposite. Someone enters, and the entire atmosphere shifts. The air feels heavy. Conversations stall. Without meaning to, they drain the space around them.

What you're experiencing in both cases is resonance—the invisible broadcast of a person's emotional home frequency.

Every one of us has one. It's not the temporary excitement after a great day or the slump after a bad one. Your emotional home is the baseline frequency you return to most often—the vibrational address you "live" at, whether you're conscious of it or not.

And here's the life-changing truth: the universe doesn't respond to your occasional peaks of positivity. It responds to your dominant frequency.

> "You don't attract what you want. You attract what
> you are." — D. Knox

The Quantum of Emotions

Emotions aren't random moods. They are measurable frequencies.

Quantum mechanics tells us that vibration attracts vibration. What you resonate with inside, you magnetize outside.

That's why two people can pray the same prayer, speak the same affirmation, or set the same goal—and yet create completely different results. One is rooted in gratitude, the other in fear. One resonates with worthiness, the other with shame. The words may match, but the frequency behind them does not.

It's not effort that creates alignment. It's resonance.

> "Your emotional home is the address where life
> forwards its mail." — D. Knox

The Thought–Emotion Loop

Here's the hidden mechanism that keeps most people stuck: the loop.

- o Thought sparks emotion.
- o Emotion fuels behavior
- o Behavior reinforces the thought.
- o And the cycle repeats.

From the outside, it looks like "just life." But beneath the surface, it's resonance on repeat.

Science explains it this way:

- A thought creates an electrical signal in the brain.
- That signal releases chemicals in the body.
- Those chemicals generate an emotion.
- The emotion radiates a magnetic field.
- Together, thought (electrical) + emotion (magnetic) = vibration.

That vibration becomes your broadcast. And the field mirrors it back—not as reward or punishment, but with mathematical precision.

This is why you can meditate in the morning, but if you spend the rest of the day replaying fear, anger, or resentment, your loop overrides your practice.

> "Your life doesn't echo your occasional highs—it reflects your constant frequency." — D. Knox

My Turning Point

I realized this when my walls were covered with affirmations, my journals full of declarations—yet my results didn't match. I was saying one thing, but broadcasting another.

On the surface, my words were hopeful. Underneath, my frequency was drenched in defeat and regret. That invisible signal was louder than anything I said.

That was my wake-up call: if I wanted a different life, I couldn't just talk differently. I had to live in a new emotional home.

Breaking the Loop: Calibration Practices

The good news? You don't have to leap from despair to bliss overnight. You calibrate. Step by step, you climb into higher states until a new emotional home becomes a natural part of you.

Gratitude + Discipline

Gratitude lifts your state upward. Discipline keeps it steady.

When I felt myself spiraling, I replaced my loops with identity-based truths:

- "I accept this moment."
- "I trust the unseen is working for me."
- "I am growing stronger every day."

Then I backed those words with discipline:

- Body > Movement and clean food proved to my body: we are rising.
- Mind > Journaling reframed toxic thoughts.
- Spirit > Gratitude and prayer tuned me to possibility.

"Gratitude collapses timelines. Discipline steadies the frequency. Together, they create alignment." — D. Knox

Stop–Swap–Speak 2.0

Here's the upgraded version for breaking loops:

Stop > Catch the thought mid-stream.

Swap > Replace it with a higher-frequency truth.

Speak > Declare it aloud and anchor it with action.

Breathe: Three deep breaths calm the nervous system.

Recall: Bring up a memory of joy or love. Feel it fully.

Shift: Change your posture. Stand tall, move, smile.

Broadcast: Imagine your higher self. What signal would they radiate? Send that.

"Every reset is a rehearsal for the life you are stepping into."
— D. Knox

Real-Life Loop Shifts

- ○ Loop: Rejection

    Thought > "Nobody ever chooses me."

    Shift > "Rejection isn't proof of unworthiness—it's redirection to alignment."

- ○ Loop: Money Stress

    Thought > "I never have enough." Shift > "I live in a universe of supply. Resources flow as I align."

- ○ Loop: Self-Doubt

    Thought > "I'll mess this up."

Shift > "I am growing. Every step builds courage and confidence."

Case Study: Marcus

Marcus came to me carrying what he called "constant pressure." On paper, he was successful—a career, family, stability. But underneath, he was burning out.

Through Awareness Mapping, we uncovered his emotional home: pressure and frustration.

We Built a Shift Script:

"I release the weight. Today, I lead from calm strength."

Then I gave him actionable steps:

- Morning Reset: Instead of reaching for his phone, Marcus started with breathwork and three simple priorities.
- Observer Practice: At lunch, he slowed down, ate without rushing, and made an effort to be present.
- Movement Commitment: I asked him to choose something for himself—something that lifted his energy. He chose the gym. He joined and committed to working out three days a week.

At first, these seemed small. But small shifts create new frequencies. Soon, his nervous system began to reset. He said "no" more often. He delegated more. He ended his days with energy instead of exhaustion.

Most importantly, his emotional home moved. He no longer lived at the address of pressure and anxiety. He shifted into peace and clarity. And once he changed homes, life began to meet him there.

> "It's not about conquering Rome overnight. It's about consistent shifts, becoming the observer, and raising your home frequency. When you do, the universe works in concert with you." — D. Knox

Living the Practice

Calibration doesn't mean you'll never feel low again. Sadness, anger, fear—they're part of being human.

The difference is this: you don't build a house there anymore. You visit, then you shift.

By mapping emotions, writing Shift Scripts, and anchoring higher states, your emotional thermostat resets. You begin to spend more time in gratitude, courage, and love than in fear or shame.

When your emotional home rises, opportunities, relationships, and blessings find themselves at your new address.

> "Your emotional home determines the neighborhood of your reality." — D. Knox

Key Takeaways

○ Emotions are frequencies that broadcast into the field.

○ Everyone has an emotional home—the vibrational set point to which they return most often.

○ The Thought–Emotion Loop explains why we stay stuck.

- Gratitude and discipline stabilize higher states.

- Stop–Swap–Speak 2.0 + Reset interrupts loops and recalibrate your frequency.

- Small, consistent steps (like Marcus's routine and workouts) shift your home frequency.

- Raise your emotional home, and reality rises with it.

> "You don't attract what you want—you attract what you are." — D. Knox

Detachment Without Disconnection: Learning to Care Without Carrying

Real freedom isn't shutting down. It's not building walls or pretending you don't care. Real freedom is learning to stay open-hearted without being overloaded.

That's what detachment truly is.

Not disconnection. Not numbness. Not escape.

Detachment is the art of caring deeply without carrying what isn't yours.

> "Self-love isn't just affirmations. Its boundaries. It's alignment. It's saying no without guilt." — D. Knox

The Burden of Expectations

For many people, one of the heaviest weights they carry isn't loss or heartbreak—it's expectation.

From childhood, families, cultures, and communities paint

pictures of who we're supposed to be. They tell us what kind of work to pursue, what type of partner to choose, and what success should look like. Some of these expectations are well-meaning, but when we take them on without discernment, they fracture our authenticity.

Living under expectation can feel like wearing a suit two sizes too small. Outwardly, you may look "put together," but inwardly, you're suffocating.

> "Carrying someone else's dream is the fastest way to silence your own." — D. Knox

Love Without Carrying

For me, the carrying showed up in my marriage and my family life.

I often absorbed the emotions of others, adjusting my own boundaries so that the people I loved could feel happy—even if it left me depleted. I carried what they thought, how they felt, and how they would react.

In marriage, this was to my own demise. I thought protecting my partner from pain meant taking it on myself. I thought love meant carrying her weight. But in doing so,

I stopped honoring my own truth. I crossed boundaries I should have held, and in the process, I weakened both of us.

The same pattern played out with my children at times. Wanting to keep the peace and ensure they were happy, I bent myself in ways that cost me coherence.

Here's the paradox I eventually realized: when you carry

someone else's lessons, you block them from the very growth their soul is calling them toward. And at the same time, you weigh yourself down with energy that isn't yours—leaving you drained, misaligned, and unable to walk in your own resonance.

True love isn't carrying. Its presence. It's walking beside someone in compassion, while trusting them to walk their own path. And when you release their weight, you free both of you: they step into their growth, and you remain aligned in your energy and purpose.

> "Love doesn't mean carrying another's burdens. Love means standing clear in your own frequency so others can rise in theirs." — D. Knox

The Weight We Are Conditioned to Carry

Caring is natural. Carrying is conditioning.

For men, society often equates worth with provision, protection, and endless responsibility.

For women, conditioning often emphasizes nurturing to the point of self-erasure.

Different roles. Same weight.

We confuse caring with exhaustion. We confuse love with sacrifice. However, the truth is that you can nurture without losing yourself. You can provide without collapsing. You can love without carrying.

Detachment vs. Disconnection

The difference is subtle but life-changing.

Healthy Detachment (What We Want):

- You care, but you no longer control outcomes.
- You stay connected, but you aren't responsible for someone else's reactions
- You observe emotions, but don't let them dictate your identity.

Mantras:

- "I can love you and still choose me."
- "I can care without carrying."

Unhealthy Disconnection (What We Release):

- Shutting down or withdrawing to avoid pain.
- Numbing out or becoming hyper-defensive.
- Believing disconnection = strength, when really it's avoidance.

Trap Thoughts:

- "If I don't detach completely, I'll get hurt again."
- "If I stop managing their feelings, they'll think I don't care."

The Quantum Weight of Attachment

At the quantum level, carrying creates entanglement.

Every time you shoulder someone else's emotions or expectations, your frequency becomes intertwined with theirs. The result is static.

The field doesn't read your good intentions—it reads your signal. And a cluttered signal mirrors back confusion, heaviness, and delay.

Detachment clears the static. It sharpens your frequency. And here's the beauty: when you release what isn't yours, you not only empower the other person to grow, but you also reclaim your own energy. You walk lighter, freer, more aligned with your true resonance—and that attracts opportunities and relationships in harmony with who you really are.

> "You don't help people by carrying them. You help them by standing clear in your own frequency." — D. Knox

Practical Reframes

"I don't want them to think I'm a bad person."

"Their interpretation is not my responsibility. I'm clear, I'm kind, I'm aligned."

"I don't want to let them down."

"Disappointing someone doesn't mean I've done wrong. I'm honoring my energy."

"They need me."

"People have their own divine guidance. I can support, but I don't have to save."

"If I detach, I'll lose them."

"If I must abandon myself to keep them, I've already lost me."

The Stop–Study–Select Practice

A simple tool to release what isn't yours:

- ○ Stop > Notice the guilt, pressure, or exhaustion.
- ○ Study > Ask: "Whose energy is this? Family? Partner? Society?"
- ○ Select > Release it with intention: "I return this energy to its rightful place. I reclaim my own field." I select the energetic timeline that is in alignment with me,

Thought Reprogramming

Grab your journal.

1. Write down the thought that ties you to someone else's emotions.
2. Create a mantra that reclaims your energy.

Examples:

- ○ Old Thought: "They'll be mad at me."
- ○ *Mantra: "I am not responsible for another's reaction to my truth."*
- ○ Old Thought: "They'll think I don't care."
- ○ *Mantra: "I care deeply, but I will not carry what isn't mine."*
- ○ Old Thought: "I feel guilty pulling back."

○   *Mantra: "Guilt is not guidance. Alignment is."*

Repeat it aloud three times. Write it daily until it feels natural.

The Balloon Visualization

Purpose: To let go of entanglements while staying open-hearted.

Close your eyes. Imagine holding a bunch of helium balloons. Each one represents an attachment—someone's expectation, a fear, a responsibility that isn't yours.

Feel the strings. Notice the weight of gripping them. You've done your part. You've shown up. But now it's time to release.

Gently let them go, one by one, saying:

"I release you with love. I return your energy to you and reclaim my own."

The balloons rise. You remain grounded—still loving, still present, but free.

Bonus Exercise: Do the balloon exercise outside with real balloons and write what you want to release on the balloons with a sharpie.

Daily Detachment Rituals

- Breathwork Reset > Three deep inhales and exhales, silently saying: "Release."

- Boundary Building > Practice saying no without guilt. No to family expectations that drain you. No to carrying others' loads.

- Water Visualization > Use a shower or running water to symbolize release. Let it wash away what isn't yours.

Key Takeaways

- Detachment is not disconnection. It's caring without carrying.

- Carrying others' expectations or emotions creates static in your frequency.

- Love isn't measured by how much you carry but by how clearly you stand.

- Society conditions men to provide, and women through nurture—but true alignment is discernment, not exhaustion.

- Detachment frees both sides: it allows others to grow, and it restores your energy, keeping you aligned in your resonance.

- Tools like reframes, mantras, Stop–Study–Select, and visualization anchor this practice.

"I release what is not mine to hold. I honor others without abandoning myself. I remain present, loving, and free." — D. Knox

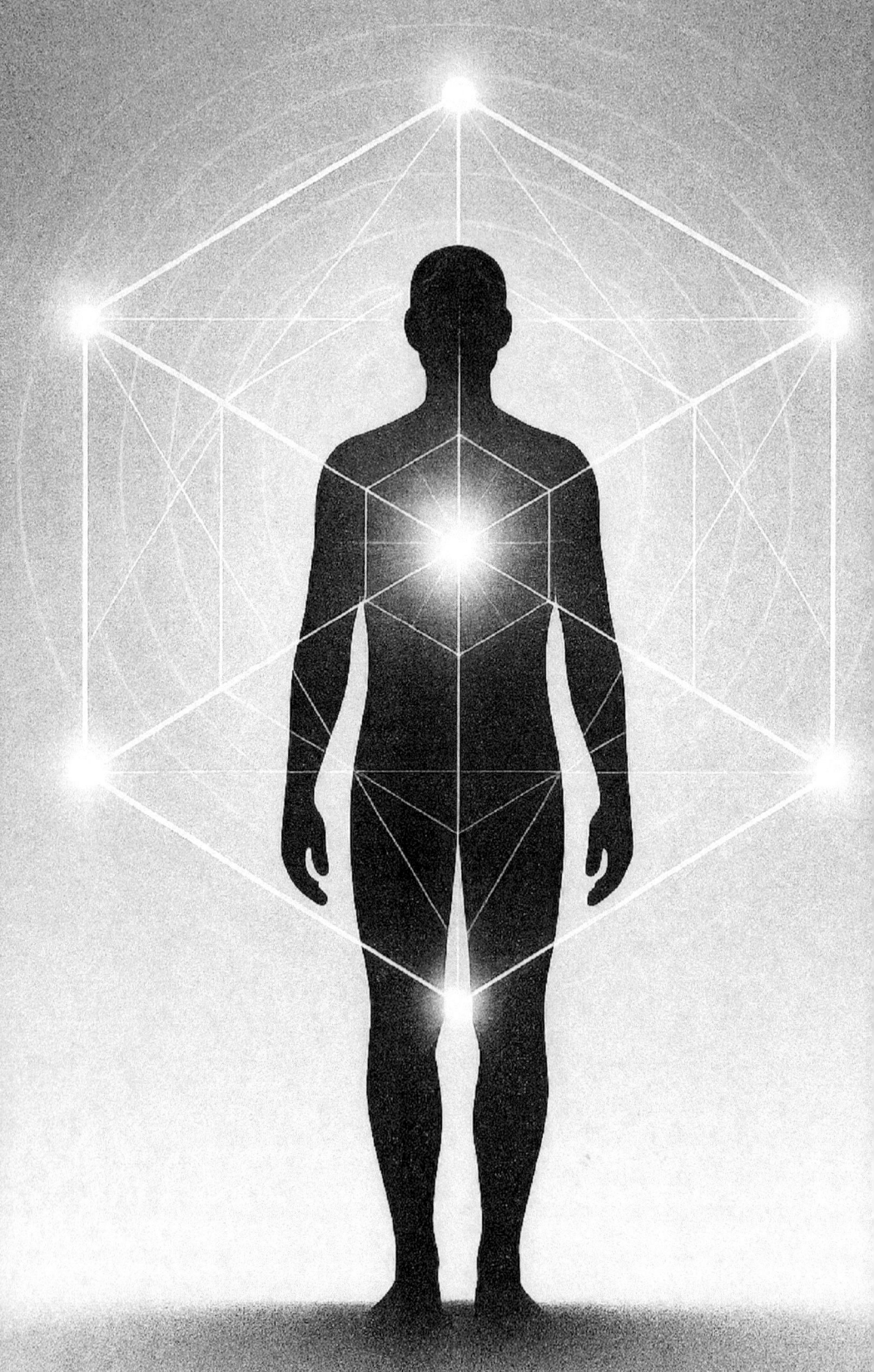

Quantum Boundaries: The Framework That Holds Your Identity

Detachment freed my heart. Boundaries built the framework to protect it.

Without boundaries, you leak energy. You say yes when you mean no. You tolerate what drains you. And little by little, you slide back into the old version of yourself.

With boundaries, you hold your resonance. You keep your energy clean. You anchor your new identity.

> "Boundaries are not just about keeping others out. They are the invisible lines that keep you in alignment with yourself."
> — D. Knox

Why "Quantum Boundaries"

In quantum physics, everything begins at the smallest level—protons, electrons, and atoms. A slight shift at the quantum level can lead to significant changes at the physical level.

The same is true for your life. Boundaries aren't just the big, dramatic choices, like leaving a job or ending a relationship. They live in the micro-decisions you make daily—the smallest acts of self-respect that accumulate into a completely new reality.

Quantum boundaries are about setting those clear energetic lines—small and large—that contain your frequency, protect your alignment, and keep you coherent in your new identity.

"One strong boundary can change your entire vibration."
— D. Knox

The Quantum Physics of Boundaries

In quantum systems, boundary conditions dictate how energy behaves. Without them, particles scatter. Systems destabilize. Energy collapses into chaos.

With boundaries, energy holds form. It organizes. It creates order, coherence, and clarity.

Your life works the same way. Without clear boundaries, your energy scatters into chaos. With boundaries, you hold your signal steady and amplify the reality you are building.

The Psychology of Boundaries

Psychologists have long shown that boundaries are essential for mental health. Weak boundaries breed resentment, burnout, and a loss of identity. Strong boundaries build self-respect, safety, and mutual trust.

○ Internal Boundaries > commitments you set with yourself.

- o External Boundaries > limits you set with others.
- o Energetic Boundaries > filters for what media, conversations, and environments you allow into your frequency.

Boundaries don't distance you from people. They elevate relationships. When people see you respect yourself, they learn to respect you more deeply.

Technique: STOP • SIFT • SELECT (Boundary Decision Triad)

When a request comes in—or a decision lands—most people react from habit, guilt, or urgency.

creates a short gap so you can respond from alignment instead of autopilot.

STOP

Take one slow breath. You don't owe anyone an instant answer.

Use this line: "Thanks for asking—let me check my capacity and get right back to you."

SIFT

Alignment: Does this honor my **values, goals,** and **new identity?**

Motive: Am I saying yes to **please/appease**, or to **align?**

Cost: What energy, time, or attention does this require? What displaces if I say yes?

Both/And: Can I honor **them** in a way that also honors me (adjust scope, timing, or terms)?

If the answer serves others **and** still serves you, it's aligned. Boundaries aren't selfish—they're truthful.

SELECT

Choose the clean move. Make one clear decision and communicate it simply.

Aligned YES (with terms): "Yes—here's what I can do by Friday."

Aligned NO (with care): "I'm not available for that, but here's an alternative that could work."

Aligned NEGOTIATE: "I can help if we shift the deadline/role/ scope."
In short you are evaluation **Value~ Energy~ Capacity**

Stop. Breathe. Sift. Check values, motive, and cost. Select. Choose the single aligned response and state it clearly.

Micro-Example

A friend asks for last-minute help.

Stop: "Let me check my day."

Sift: Value = generosity ($\checkmark$), Energy = already low (X), Capacity = partial (Δ).

Select: "I can give you 20 minutes now or an hour tomorrow— what's better?"

Remember: Boundaries are not walls; they're truthful edges that keep your commitments, energy, and identity intact. **STOP • SIFT • SELECT** makes your decisions intentional—so your calendar tells the same truth as your core.

"Above all else, guard your heart, for everything you do flows from it." — Proverbs 4:23

#1 Self Boundaries

The most Important boundary starts with setting boundaries for yourself! Honor yourself first to make boundaries with others seamless

My Story: Boundaries Saved My Alignment

When I began walking into my new identity, one thing became clear: without boundaries, I would slip back into my old self.

So I began drawing new lines:

- With my ex > limiting communication so I wouldn't get pulled back into loops.
- In business > no more late payments without consequence, no more deals that drained my peace.
- With family > clarifying respect, responsibility, and space in my home.
- With myself > honoring my body, my environment, my goals, and my time.

On a micro-level, I created small but powerful rules:

- I will not start my day by reaching for my phone or scrolling social media.
- I will begin every morning with gratitude.
- I will pause before committing to anything

These weren't restrictions. They were lines of freedom. Every time I honored a boundary, I felt my identity stabilize. Every time I broke one, I felt myself slide backward.

"Every 'no' you speak from alignment is a 'yes' to your higher self." — D. Knox

Macro & Micro Self Boundaries

Both matter—because both shape your resonance.

Macro Self Boundaries (the big ones):

- I will not tolerate disrespect.
- I will not sacrifice my values to appease others.
- I will not enter business deals that compromise my peace.

Micro Self Boundaries (the daily ones):

- I will not start my day in distraction.
- I will not absorb gossip, toxic talk, or negative media.
- I will pause before reacting emotionally
- I will give myself time to think before saying yes.

Macro boundaries stop obvious chaos. Micro boundaries keep your frequency clean.Together, they create the scaffolding that holds your identity.

"Boundaries don't just protect your energy. They design your reality." — D. Knox

Boundaries & Your Resonant Home

Here's why this matters: your emotional home frequency—the baseline vibration you live in—depends on boundaries.

Without them, other people's chaos becomes your signal. You take on their burdens. You live in their static. And the field mirrors it all back to you.

With boundaries, you stay in your chosen frequency. You broadcast clarity, self-respect, and coherence. And life responds to that signal.

"Your emotional home is the address where life forwards its mail. Boundaries keep you living at the right address." — D. Knox

Reflection: Quantum Boundary Audit

Take time to observe. Write down your answers:

○ Where did my old self lack boundaries that my new self must protect?

○ Where do I need micro-boundaries to stay aligned?

○ Who in my life needs new boundaries to keep our relationship balanced?

○ Am I saying yes out of love, or out of guilt and fear?

○ What would it feel like to fully respect my own energy?

Clarity is freedom. The more specific you become, the stronger your resonance will be.

Key Takeaways

○ Boundaries = coherence. They keep your frequency clean and strong.

○ Without them, your new identity collapses into old patterns.

- Boundaries exist on every level: internal, external, and energetic.
- Macro boundaries stop obvious chaos. Micro boundaries reshape daily frequency.
- Boundaries transform relationships. They teach others how to value and respect you.
- Boundaries protect your resonant home frequency and keep you from backsliding.

> "Boundaries are not walls. They are the framework that lets love, respect, and alignment flow freely." — D. Knox

Quantum Forgiveness: Releasing the Weight, Opening the Portal

There is no gateway more critical on the path to identity alignment than forgiveness.

You can set boundaries, master rituals, and practice affirmations—but if you still carry the weight of resentment, guilt, or shame, you remain tethered to your old self. Unforgiveness is the invisible chain that anchors people in the past, holding their vibration in a frequency too low for their new self to emerge.

Forgiveness is not about pretending it didn't happen. It is not excusing betrayal, injustice, or disappointment. Forgiveness is quantum release. It is the act of collapsing an old probability—of letting go of the wave of pain—so that new frequencies of freedom can come into form.

"Forgiveness is not about them. It is about freeing you."
— D. Knox

The Quantum Mechanics of Forgiveness

Quantum mechanics reveals that energy is never lost, but rather transferred. When we replay betrayal, disappointment, or guilt, we recycle that same energy through our body, our mind, and the field. That resonance attracts more of what we don't want, amplifying pain instead of possibility.

Unforgiveness is not just an emotional wound—it is a broadcast. It saturates your resonant home frequency with static, keeping you magnetized to old outcomes.

But forgiveness clears the channel. It collapses the loop of suffering and makes space for new frequencies to take root.

Science confirms what mystics always knew: holding onto resentment floods the nervous system with cortisol, suppresses the immune system, and rewires the brain for vigilance and fear. According to Dr. Everett Worthington, a leading researcher on forgiveness, unforgiveness is associated with chronic stress, high blood pressure, and even increased risk of disease. Spiritually, it blocks blessings. Energetically, it chains you to the old self.

Forgiveness, then, is not just moral. It is mechanical. It is the vibrational reset button for your soul.

> "Resentment is a prison. Forgiveness is the key that opens the door." — D. Knox

Forgiving Yourself First

The heaviest weight we carry is often not what others did to us—but what we did to ourselves.

You must forgive yourself for not knowing then what you know now.

Forgive yourself for the boundaries you abandoned, the dreams you delayed, the health you neglected, the moments you chose survival over truth.

Mistakes were not failures—they were part of the curriculum. Every detour held a lesson. Every collapse was preparation.

As Jesus prayed: "Father, forgive them, for they know not what they do." (Luke 23:34)

That applies to you too. You were learning, growing, experimenting with life. You did the best you could with the tools available to you. Now, with wisdom, you can release the old shame and step into new strength.

> "Failure is not the opposite of growth. It is the curriculum." — D. Knox

Forgiving Others

After self-forgiveness comes the release of others.

- Parents who projected their dreams onto you.
- Partners who betrayed you.
- Friends who abandoned you.
- The family who judged you.

Forgiveness doesn't mean reconciliation—it means liberation. You don't have to invite them back into your life to stop carrying them in your soul.

From a quantum perspective, these people were not random

villains in your story. They were teachers. mirrors. catalysts. The Law of Attraction brought them into your orbit so that your soul could grow, expand, and realign.

The Qur'an reminds us: "Repel evil with that which is better, and your enemy will become as close as an intimate friend." (41:34)

To forgive is to sever the karmic contract and free yourself to vibrate at a higher level.

> "They were not detours. They were directions." — D. Knox

Case Study: John's Release

Take John, one of my clients. He grew up in a home filled with challenges. His father wasn't around. His mother—doing her best as a single parent—battled depression and addiction. John had to grow up fast, fending for himself while watching other kids live the middle-class stability he longed for.

But here's the paradox: while the pain and chaos shaped him, it also lit a fire. It pushed him to excel in school, to dominate in sports, and to aim higher than the circumstances he was handed.

Still, as he grew into adulthood, the wounds followed him. Feelings of abandonment. Resentment. The quiet ache of not having the support every child deserves.

Through our work together, John began to reframe his past. He realized the very cards he had been dealt had also given him resilience, determination, and strength most people never build. What he once saw as a disadvantage had actually become preparation.

The breakthrough came when John chose forgiveness. He

forgave his mother—not excusing her addiction, but releasing her from the weight he had carried for years. He saw her humanity, her struggles, and let go of the anger that had been blocking his peace.

He forgave his father, too, understanding that the failure of his parents' marriage didn't mean a failure of love. In fact, John reconnected with his dad, and they built a relationship stronger than he ever thought possible.

That release changed everything. John stopped living in the shadow of resentment. His frequency lifted. His energy shifted from survival to thriving. Today, John excels in everything he touches— not because his past disappeared, but because forgiveness freed him from carrying it forward.

Here's the lesson: forgiveness doesn't mean letting people "off the hook." It means releasing yourself from the hook you've been caught on. Everyone has their own path, their own battles, their own vortex of challenges. Forgiveness is recognizing that what was placed in front of you was not punishment, but shaping. It was forging you for your mission in this lifetime.

"Nothing is happening to you. It's happening for you." — D. Knox

Micro-Forgiveness: Clearing the Small Loops

Not all forgiveness is about monumental betrayals. Some of the most toxic weight comes from the daily micro-loops we ignore:

- ○ The guilt of skipping your ritual.
- ○ The sting of snapping at a child or partner.
- ○ The regret of saying "yes" when you meant "no."

○   The shame of not showing up as your best self.

These micro-wounds accumulate. They slowly drag your frequency downward until heaviness feels normal. Forgiveness here is just as vital. Clear the static daily before it calcifies into identity.

> "Forgive in real time. Don't let small wounds turn
> into scars." — D. Knox

The Forgiveness Framework

Forgive Yourself

Write down the ways you've judged yourself. Reframe them as lessons. Bless the version of you who did what they knew at the time. Also understand that every challage, let down, disappointment and even trauma was part of your life path to shape you who you are today. The key is to see those circumstances differently. Go back and reframe those experiences and pull the silver linings out. Think of who you are today and would you be that person without those experiences?

Forgive Others

List the people or situations that still trigger anger or sadness. Next to each name, write: "I release you with love. You were part of my becoming."

Forgive Life

Sometimes it's not people—it's circumstances. The job you lost. The illness you endured. The breakup you didn't expect. Forgive the process. Reframe the collapse as the soil for your expansion.

Anchor the Release

Don't keep it in your head—speak it aloud. Breathe it into your body. Pair it with movement, prayer, or ritual. Feel the heaviness leave your cells as you declare the release.

> "Unforgiveness is the static in your broadcast.
> Forgiveness clears the channel." — D. Knox

Self-Reflection: The Observer of Release

Pause. Breathe deeply. Act now as the observer of your frequency.

What grudges, large or small, am I still carrying in my body?

Where am I punishing myself for past mistakes instead of learning from them?

Who do I silently blame for my current state?

What emotion do I feel when I think of that person or situation—and what would it feel like if I released it?

If my soul's expansion required every disappointment I've experienced, can I bless the role they played in my becoming?

Let these questions sit with you. Not to judge—but to clarify. Because the field is always listening. And your resonant home will always call your reality.

Journal Practice: Three Levels of Forgiveness

Tonight, take out your journal. Divide the page into three simple headings:

Self — Write down the ways you need to forgive yourself. Where have you been harsh, critical, or unloving toward yourself? Release the judgment. Replace it with compassion.

Others — Write the names of those who hurt you. Next to each, write one sentence of release. You don't have to send it to them. This is for you.

Life — Write the situations that broke your heart, the disappointments that still sting. Reframe them as training grounds. Write: "This was not punishment. This was preparation."

Let the ink itself become release. By writing it, you are broadcasting a new frequency into the field.

> "Forgiveness is the portal to freedom. Step through it, and the future unfolds." — D. Knox

Quantum Forgiveness Challenge

Wisdom without practice is potential left unrealized. Forgiveness only reshapes your life when you live it. So here's your challenge:

Write down four specific acts of forgiveness—two micro and two macro.

Step 1: Start Small (Micro-Forgiveness)

Choose two small things you can forgive right now. It could be:

- Forgive yourself for not keeping a commitment and recommit to it this week.
- Forgiving a coworker or acquaintance for something minor but lingering.

   ○   Forgiving yourself for snapping, skipping a ritual, or saying "yes" when you meant "no."

These may feel small, but the energy they free up is powerful. Each micro-forgiveness is like clearing static from your broadcast signal.

Step 2: Go Deeper (Macro-Forgiveness)

Now, choose two larger things you've been holding onto. These could be:

   ○   A parent who let you down.

   ○   A partner who betrayed you.

   ○   A friend who abandoned you.

   ○   A circumstance that scarred you.

Reframe it. See where you can give grace, even if it's only the grace of acknowledging: "They were operating at the vibration they had at the time." Or perhaps: "They were wrong, but I will not let that wrong define me."

Release them. Reclaim yourself. Let the lesson remain but let the burden go.

Step 3: Anchor the Energy

Speak your four releases out loud. Declare:

"I release you with love. I reclaim my energy. I walk free."

Feel the lightness enter your body as you say it. That shift is not imagined—it is measurable. Forgiveness raises your frequency, and the field responds.

"Forgiveness is not weakness. It is frequency work. It frees your energy to create the future you deserve." — D. Knox

Key Takeaways

- Forgiveness is a gateway to identity alignment. You can master rituals and boundaries, but if resentment remains, you're still tethered to the old self.

- It's not excusing the past—it's releasing it. Forgiveness collapses the old loop of pain so a new frequency (freedom) can take form.

- Unforgiveness is a broadcast. It saturates your "home frequency" with static, keeping you magnetized to old outcomes; forgiveness clears the channel.

- Self-forgiveness comes first. You did the best you could with the tools you had. Reframe mistakes as curriculum and retrieve your energy from shame.

- Forgiving others = liberation, not reconciliation. Release the karmic contract; you don't have to re-enter relationship to stop carrying them.

- Everyone was a catalyst. What looked like detours were directions—teachers and mirrors for your becoming.

- Micro-forgiveness matters. Clear small loops (missed rituals, short tempers, misaligned yeses) before they calcify into identity.

- A practical framework helps you anchor it. Forgive Self, Forgive Others, Forgive Life—then speak the release and pair it with breath, prayer, or movement.

- Frequency follows forgiveness. As you release, your nervous system, energy, and results rise into alignment.

- Live it, don't just learn it. Choose two micro and two macro releases; speak them aloud: "I release you with love. I reclaim my energy. I walk free."

Environmental Frequency Cleanse: Creating Space for Your Becoming

When I began rebuilding my life, I had a realization that shifted everything: I was doing the inner work, but my outer environment was still rehearsing the past.

No matter how many affirmations I spoke, how much gratitude I practiced, or how consistent my routines were, my environment was broadcasting a different story. The photos on my walls whispered old memories. The furniture carried the weight of relationships I had already outgrown. Even the music in my car pulled me back into frequencies I was trying to escape.

It hit me: my environment wasn't neutral. It was a broadcast. And if I wanted to live as my new identity, I couldn't keep surrounding myself with the leftovers of my old one.

"You can't step into the new you while surrounding yourself with echoes of the old you." — D. Knox

The Quantum of Environment

Quantum physics teaches us that energy is everywhere—nothing is static. Every object, every scent, every sound vibrates and carries memory. Over time, your environment becomes like a mirror, constantly reflecting back the version of you that lived it.

Psychologists call this contextual priming—your brain links environments to emotions and behaviors. Walk into the same cluttered room, and your nervous system replays the same moods. Sit at the same desk with the same piles of paper, and your focus dips into the same stress. Without changing the environment, your frequency defaults to the past.

That's why environmental shifts matter. They aren't cosmetic. They're quantum. They reset the vibrational field within which you live.

> "Clutter is the residue of indecision. Order is the language of alignment." — D. Knox

Cleaning the Outer Temple

Your home, your car, and your workspace are your three loudest transmitters. They either anchor your new self or rehearse your old one.

When I was rebuilding, I decluttered my home. I let go of photos, clothes, and objects tied to my past relationship. I couldn't replace everything, but I made intentional shifts—new scents in the air, fresh furniture pieces, a clean workspace that reflected who I was becoming.

I cleaned out my car and swapped my playlists for high-frequency music that calmed my nervous system. The transformation was immediate. Walking into my home, stepping into my car, or sitting at my desk no longer triggered old stories. Instead, each space became a rehearsal room for my future.

> "Environment is the rehearsal space of destiny." — D. Knox

No Contact, No Carrying

When a bond has become draining or chaotic, **no contact** isn't punishment—it's a **reset protocol**. It pauses the cycle long enough for your mind, body, and spirit to find level ground again. Think of it as stepping out of turbulent water so your balance returns.

Why "no contact"? Because every point of connection carries signal. Even a text has frequency. A quick phone call can reopen emotional loops you're trying to close. This is more than a heartbreak strategy—it's a **quantum reset** that stops the energetic bleed and protects your baseline.

The Science + The Field:

Relationships tangled in toxicity, blame, or dependence lower your **home frequency**. Neuroscience shows that hearing a familiar voice or seeing a face from your past can trigger the **same chemical cascades** you had together—memory encoded in biology. Without a break, your nervous system keeps predicting the old story.

Why solitude matters:

Solitude gives your spirit space to reset, your nervous system time to establish a **new baseline**, and your frequency room to **recalibrate**. In the quiet, God—Source, Spirit, the Field—can finally be heard.

My proof:

After my breakup, I rushed into another relationship. My baseline hadn't reset, and it showed. Only when I gave myself nearly a year to declutter, heal, and deepen my spiritual practice did my strength return. That season also birthed **Quantum Identity Alignment™.**

Bottom line:

No contact = no carrying. Protect your signal, let the chemistry settle, and step into the identity you're choosing—on purpose.

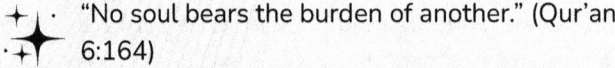 "No soul bears the burden of another." (Qur'an 6:164)

"Come out from among them and be separate." (2 Corinthians 6:17)

The Sensory Broadcast

The environment isn't just physical. It's sensory.

- Music > Songs aren't harmless background noise. They're emotional triggers. If you're healing, replaying "your song" with an ex keeps you bound. Switch to frequencies that uplift—instrumentals, calming tones, or joyful beats that open your spirit.

- Media > Social feeds, TV, podcasts—these are mental diets. Gossip, chaos, and fear tune your nervous system to a state of scarcity. Inspiration, wisdom, and stories of growth tune it to abundance.

- Conversations > Words carry frequency. If you spend hours around negativity, criticism, or gossip, those vibrations shape your thoughts and behavior. Protect your circle. Choose life-giving voices.

 "Do not be misled: bad company corrupts good character." (1 Corinthians 15:33)

Bonus Practices for Environmental Alignment

Here are practical ways to reprogram your environment for the identity you're stepping into:

Audible & Audiobooks > Replace empty noise with intentional input. Listen to teachings, stories, or wisdom that mirror your future self. Feed your ears with your becoming. I personally replace music in car rides with a good audibled or while working out.

Nighttime Frequency Programming > Before bed, play high-frequency Hertz music (432 Hz, 528 Hz, or binaural beats). As your brain enters theta, your subconscious absorbs the vibration, rewriting patterns while you sleep.

Crystal & Scent Anchors > Use anchors to remind your nervous system of peace and alignment. A crystal on your desk, lavender oil in the evening, or a candle during journaling. Over time, your senses will become accustomed to these sensations, associating them with clarity and calm.

> "Every sense is a doorway. Guard the doors of your becoming." — D. Knox

Self-Reflection Frequency Audit

Take a deep breath. Look—not just with your eyes, but with your awareness.

What in my home, car, or workspace still echoes yesterday? What deserves to be released so I can breathe in newness?

Who in my circle drains my energy or entangles me in loops I'm ready to break? Do I need distance—or no contact—to reset my baseline?

What music, media, or conversations am I consuming daily? Do they align with my new identity, or a rehearse of my past?

What anchors of light—symbols, scents, sounds—can I bring in to remind me of who I'm becoming?

These aren't chores. They're invitations. Invitations to curate your outer world so it no longer betrays your inner one.

 "Be not conformed to this world, but be transformed by the renewing of your mind." (Romans 12:2)

Key Takeaways

- ○ Your environment is never neutral—it broadcasts frequency.
- ○ Home, car, workspace, media, and relationships all shape your baseline.
- ○ No contact and solitude create the space for a new frequency to form.
- ○ Sensory inputs—such as music, conversations, and media— are just as important as physical objects.
- ○ Small environmental shifts create powerful vibrational resets.
- ○ Alignment begins outside as much as it does within.

"Everything around you is catching up to your alignment. Release what echoes the old you and make room for who you are becoming." — D. Knox

Quantum Rituals: Locking in the New You

Most people think transformation happens in a single lightning-strike moment: a breakthrough at a seminar, a spiritual awakening in meditation, or a sudden flash of clarity that changes everything.

But here's the truth: moments inspire—rituals transform.

Moments create sparks, but rituals build fires. Transformation lasts not because of what happens once, but because of what you repeat.

I learned this the hard way. I'd leave big events or powerful workshops feeling energized and unstoppable. For a week, I was on fire. But then daily life pressed in, distractions crept back, and the spark dimmed. Again and again, I wondered, 'Why do I keep losing momentum?'

The answer came clear: inspiration without integration doesn't stick. Unless you create rituals to carry the spark, the flame fades.

"Routines are what you do. Rituals are who you become." — D. Knox

Quantum mechanics teaches that energy follows attention. Whatever you focus on consistently becomes the groove reality runs through. Each repeated thought, each repeated act, carves channels of coherence in your field. Over time, those channels shape your identity.

Psychology refers to this phenomenon as neuroplasticity—your brain literally rewires itself in response to what you repeatedly practice. Rituals are not mindless habits; they are embodied signals broadcast into the field: This is who I am now.

Dr. Joe Dispenza puts it this way: "The body becomes the mind." When you attach movement to intention, thought to action, your body begins to remember your future self—even when your old mind wants to drag you back.

That's why rituals matter. They are quantum anchors—turning inspiration into embodiment, thought into frequency, and frequency into reality.

Gratitude in Motion

For me, gratitude became one of the most powerful rituals in my transformation.

Each morning, before I reached for my phone or started my workday, I spoke gratitude out loud. Sometimes I would weave gratitude into workouts—repeating affirmations of thanks with each lift or every step of a walk.

Why? Because gratitude is one of the highest frequencies. It shifts energy faster than almost anything else. Gratitude tells the universe: I already have. I already am. I am aligned.

Psychologists have confirmed that gratitude can lower depression, improve sleep, and increase resilience. Quantum physics shows gratitude collapses possibilities into form by embodying abundance before it arrives. Spiritually, gratitude is worship. Energetically, it's coherence.

> "Gratitude is the frequency that unlocks
> every door." — D. Knox

Anchoring Objects: Tangible Signals of Identity

Humanity has always used physical anchors to embody belief—such as wedding rings, prayer beads, crosses, mala necklaces, and lucky coins. Anchors are not superstition. They are reminders.

Choose an object that symbolizes your aligned self:

○ A bracelet you put on each morning, declaring: I walk in clarity and strength.

○ A pendant you touch before an important meeting: I speak with confidence and power.

○ A stone you hold in meditation: I am grounded. I am becoming.

Over time, your nervous system links the object to the state. A single touch can bring you back into coherence.

> "Anchors are not magic—they are cues. They collapse
> intention into embodiment." — D. Knox

Rituals That Rewire

Rituals don't have to be complex. Simplicity is what makes them sustainable.

○ Morning Gratitude Ritual > Before your phone, list three things you're thankful for.

- ○ Walking Affirmations > Turn walks into meditations. "I walk in clarity. I walk in love."

- ○ Mirror Ritual > Look yourself in the eyes and say: "You are already the person you've envisioned."

- ○ Evening Seal > Before bed, light a candle, breathe deeply, and declare: "Today, I walked as my higher self."

- ○ Anchor Object > Touch or wear your anchor daily: "This is my frequency. This is my new self."

The more you repeat them, the less they feel forced. Eventually, they stop being something you do and become something you are.

> "Identity doesn't shift because of what you know—it shifts because of what you rehearse." — D. Knox

Rituals Across Time

Rituals are not new. They are as old as humanity itself. From the beginning of time, people have used ritual to anchor transformation, connection, and identity.

- ○ Christianity > Prayer, fasting, worship, and Sunday gatherings recalibrate the soul.

- ○ Islam > Daily salah grounds believers five times a day in remembrance and surrender.

- ○ Buddhism > Meditation, chanting, and breath harmonize mind and body.

- ○ Judaism > Sabbath rituals create sacred rhythm and communal coherence.

- ○ Indigenous Traditions > Fire, drum, ceremony, and earth rituals align communities with nature and Spirit.

Rituals endure because they work. They are not random customs. They are technologies of alignment. They stabilize energy. They create rhythm. They turn faith into embodiment.

> "Rituals are how humanity has always remembered the divine." — D. Knox

Self-Reflection: Frequency Audit

Pause. Reflect. Ask yourself:

○ What rituals am I already practicing—conscious or unconscious?

○ Which ones align me, and which ones drain me?

○ Do I have an anchor object that connects me to my higher self?

○ What new rituals can I implement future self rehearse every day?

The answers will show you which rituals need to be created, elevated, or released.

Key Takeaways

○ Transformation doesn't last through moments—it lasts through rituals.

○ Rituals transition from the conscious to the subconscious, becoming deeply embedded in one's identity.

- ○ Gratitude, especially paired with movement, is a powerful frequency amplifier.
- ○ Anchor objects serve as daily cues for embodiment and alignment.
- ○ Rituals have always been humanity's universal tool for coherence across cultures.

"Routines are actions. Rituals are embodiment. Rituals make identity undeniable." — D. Knox

The Science of Stillness | Returning to the Zero Point

The Field Beneath Movement

Before the universe moved, it was still.

Not empty — alive with potential.

Not silent — vibrating with intelligence.

In quantum physics, this is known as the Zero Point Field — the vacuum of potential energy from which all form emerges.

Every atom, every outcome, every possibility exists there first — silent, unseen, waiting to be observed.

Stillness is that same field within you.

It's the inner equilibrium where thought softens, emotion settles, and your frequency returns to coherence with Source.

You don't retreat from life to find stillness; you allow life to slow down inside of you.

> "Stillness is not the absence of motion — it's the mastery of it." — D. Knox

The Physics of Presence

Energy responds to observation.

When the mind is chaotic, your signal scatters.

When you are still, your energy transmits a single, clear command to the Field.

Stillness is coherence — a unified vibrational state between body, mind, and spirit.

In neuroscience this mirrors Alpha and Theta brainwave states — where the hemispheres synchronize, the nervous system relaxes, and intuition heightens.

> "When you stop chasing results, results start chasing you." — D. Knox

My Journey into Stillness

There came a moment in my evolution when no more doing was required — only being.

After cycles of forgiveness, boundary work, and emotional clearing, I sensed there was one final gate: **Stillness. The Zero Point**

So I entered it, not by vanishing from the world but by changing how I moved within it.

I still had a business to run and a life to rebuild, but I disconnected from unnecessary noise — dating, over-socializing, distractions that fed my old identity.

I began to **observe instead of react**. Allowing my new self to fully integrate into my new reality that was sifting before my eyes day by day.

I paused before replying, prayed before deciding, breathed before fixing.

Some days I allowed time — even several days — to pass before responding, just to ensure my energy, not my programming, was speaking. Examining and studying life.

That was my initiation into functional stillness.

It wasn't passive; it was precise.

Each pause broke an old neural loop.

Each breath reclaimed authority from the version of me that once operated on survival.

"You cannot quantum-leap through chaos; you must calm the signal first." — D. Knox

The Shedding Stillness Awakens

As your frequency stabilizes, the universe begins reorganizing itself around your new vibration.

This is the shedding phase — the energetic purification that always follows transformation.

When your resonance rises, anything not aligned will naturally fall away.

Relationships, environments, conversations — even long-standing family ties — start to shift or dissolve. It's not rejection; it's resonance. This process is inevitable. I had lost family and friends as I moved into my new frequency and because I understood this I was able to move through it with clarity and understanding. You will reach this point as well.

> "When your frequency shifts, your cast of characters changes." — D. Knox

You may experience sudden tension, emotional breakpoints, or what feels like chaos.
Sometimes the universe will create drama or even trauma as a release valve — a way to sever connections that can't exist in your new timeline.

I lived this truth.

As I deepened in stillness, one of my closest family relationships erupted into confrontation.

My first impulse was pain — but stillness pulled me into observation.

Rather than fix the story, I studied the energy: What vibration is this conflict revealing?

That's when I saw it clearly — the universe was removing density I could no longer carry.

And once I accepted that, peace followed.

> "Sometimes the universe must create friction to finalize your freedom." — D. Knox

Shedding is sacred.

It is not loss; it is alignment.

Your task is not to hold on — it's to remain still enough to see what's truly happening.

Don't analyze the argument; witness the energy exchange.

Don't mourn what left; bless what completed.

Everything leaving is making space for what's meant to recognize your new frequency.

The Rebirth After Release

Every shedding opens a door.

As old connections fade, new ones appear — souls calibrated to your expansion.

These relationships arrive effortlessly, communicate clearly, and honor your evolution.

> "Let go with grace so the next chapter can recognize you."
> — D. Knox

Stillness keeps you steady during this recalibration. It allows the quantum intelligence to restructure your orbit without your interference.

You simply stay aligned, aware, and observant.

The Quantum Mechanism

At the subatomic level, agitation creates distortion.

Stillness restores coherence — like water settling until it mirrors the sky.

The same happens in consciousness: your clarity becomes creation's command.

When you stop reacting to the world you once created, you give birth to the one you've designed.

"You don't have to fix the old you — just stop feeding it."
— D. Knox

The Practice of Living Stillness

Stillness is a lifestyle of deliberate pace.

Here are practices that integrate it into daily movement:

Micro-Pauses: Before you speak, text, or decide — breathe.

Prayer over Pressure: Invite divine timing instead of control.

Observation Mode: Study your reactions as data, not drama.

Slow Decisions: Allow 24 hours before major responses.

Sacred Solitude: Honor quiet moments where God can recalibrate you.

Reflection & Integration

Reflection: Where do I confuse movement with momentum?

Awareness: Which relationships feel heavy when I stand still?

Practice: Can I remain silent long enough to hear divine instruction? Integration: How can I observe endings without labeling them as loss? And see the broader lesson or direction the universe is directing

Stillness is where your higher self speaks louder than the world.

It's the frequency of trust — the vibration of divine timing.

You don't find stillness by stopping life; you find it by **living deliberately.**

And once you can hold that state — even in motion — you

become untouchable by chaos.

You don't just reach peace.

You **become it.**

Key Takeaways

o Stillness is the field where creation begins and alignment is remembered.

o Calm the signal; coherence is the language the universe understands.

o Observation over reaction is the true mark of mastery.

o Shedding is sacred—release what no longer vibrates at your frequency.

o Let endings happen with grace; they're making room for resonance.

o Pause before motion; breath is the reset button of reality.

o Stillness isn't escape—it's strategy.

o Be so centered that chaos has nothing to attach to.

o In stillness, the universe recognizes your new identity.

Living the New You: Walking in Alignment

There comes a moment in every transformation when the focus shifts from becoming to being.

You've likely heard the phrase quantum leap. To some, it sounds like an abstract or magical concept. But now, after walking through this process, you understand its real meaning: a leap in identity so profound that your old self can barely recognize the life

you're living now.

You've walked the path.

You've broken the loops.

You've rewritten your language.

You've recalibrated your emotional home.

You've cleansed your environment.

You've anchored rituals to lock in the new.

And now, the moment arrives to live it.

"Alignment isn't something you chase. It's the rhythm you return to." — D. Knox

The Frequency Gates

Morning and evening are not ordinary bookends to your day. They are frequency gates—the sacred openings and closings that set the vibration for everything in between.

Morning Flow

- Daily Affirmation + Gratitude > Begin by speaking as your new identity. Anchor your words in gratitude, which magnetizes abundance.

- Hydration + Nutrition > Fuel your vessel intentionally. Water with blessing, food with light.

- Movement > Sweat clears stagnation. Every stretch, step, or lift electrifies your frequency.

- Anchor Ritual > Touch your object, mantra, or sacred symbol. Lock it in before the world makes demands.

- Reframe Check > If an old loop sneaks in, stop, swap, and speak, then reset immediately.

Evening Flow

- Release & Reframe > Empty out the day. Don't carry it into tomorrow.

- Identity Reflection > Ask: How did I show up as my aligned self today?

- Night Anchor Ritual > A candle, mantra, or prayer to seal the frequency.

- Celebrate a Win > Name one action your old self never would have done vs. your new self.

> "Your mornings declare who you are becoming. Your evenings prove who you choose to be." — D. Knox

Rhythm Over Perfection

Living in alignment doesn't mean you'll never slip. Old loops may whisper. Doubt may creep in. Low-frequency days will happen.

But alignment isn't about perfection. It's about rhythm. It's about returning faster, more consistently, and with greater ease.

Think of a musician tuning an instrument. Even the finest violin goes flat. Mastery isn't about never slipping—it's learning how to retune until harmony is restored.

> "Falling out of alignment isn't failure. Refusing to return is." — D. Knox

The Physics of Alignment

Why do rituals, journaling, gratitude, and embodiment matter so much? Because they literally rewire your brain and body into coherence.

- o Neuroplasticity > Each repeated choice carves new neural pathways.
- o Wave Collapse > Embodying your new self stabilizes one timeline into form.
- o Electromagnetic Broadcast > Thoughts are electric, emotions magnetic. Together, they broadcast coherence.

The HeartMath Institute demonstrates that coherence

strengthens immunity, focus, and intuition. Alignment isn't just spiritual—it's biological.

"Coherence collapses chaos into clarity." — D. Knox

The 14-Day Integration

For the next 14 days, end each night with these three questions:

Did I live in alignment today? √ / X

Where did I feel most aligned

Where did I feel challenged—and how did I return?

This is not about guilt. The field doesn't mirror perfection—it mirrors consistency.

Then > Now: Identity Reflection

Pause. Compare the "then" you with the "now" you.

Before: Loops, clutter, old patterns.

Now: Gratitude, coherence, and rituals anchoring your resonance.

This is your proof: you've shifted your resonant home. And when resonance shifts, reality follows.

"You've crossed into a new timeline. You are no longer becoming—you are being." — D. Knox

Closing Ceremony

Graduation deserves a ceremony. Write a letter to your old self, releasing them from the past. Or record a short message declaring who you are now. Seal it. This simple act marks the threshold: you're no longer rehearsing—you're living.

Key Takeaways

- Integration is about living, not chasing.
- Mornings and evenings are frequency gates.
- Alignment is rhythm, not perfection.
- Coherence is both spiritual and biological.
- The ceremony seals the shift—you are now living the new you.

"You don't visit alignment—you live it." — D. Knox

The Field Within the Field: Walking with Higher Consciousness

You've walked this far.

　　You've broken loops.

You've cleansed environments.

You've rewritten thought patterns.

You've learned to walk in your new identity, to align with your resonant home, to set boundaries, and to forgive.

Now we arrive at the closing threshold—the place where everything you've practiced connects with something larger than you. Something older, deeper, eternal.

Because the field—the invisible web of energy and consciousness we've been exploring—is not empty. It is intelligent. It listens. It responds. It breathes through every soul, every leaf, every star.

　　"In Him we live, and move, and have our being." — Acts 17:28

Science calls it intelligence.

Mystics call it Source.

Religions refer to it as God, Allah, Spirit, or Creator.

The name is secondary. What matters is recognition. To observe it is itself an act of alignment.

The Field Within the Field

Quantum physics shows us that everything vibrates, everything resonates, everything is connected. Yet it does not explain why the universe bends toward life, order, and renewal. Left alone, chaos should reign. And yet—life grows. Flowers bloom. Cells regenerate. Order emerges again and again.

That is the fingerprint of God-consciousness within the field.

It is the whisper that tells birds to migrate, the tide to return, your heart to beat while you sleep.

This field is not mechanical. It is relational. It responds not only to your resonance but to your surrender. You can visualize, affirm, and broadcast—but there is a higher level still: allowing the higher intelligence to meet you in the field.

 "Be still, and know that I am God." — Psalm 46:10

Spirit Guides and Angels: Companions in the Field

Within this field lives an expansive realm—the unseen companions of your journey. angels. guides. ancestors. They are not myths but real frequencies of intelligence, moving with you, helping align your steps.

You've already felt them:

That nudge that told you to turn left instead of right.

That unexpected open door you didn't even know to pray for.

That strength that rose when your strength was gone.

I've lived it myself.

When addiction had me bound, it wasn't affirmations that broke me free. It was grace.

When my business collapsed, but doors still opened, it wasn't willpower. It was favor.

When despair pressed heavily, there was a whisper, a presence, a hand unseen but undeniably real.

That was the higher intelligence of the field reaching into my life.

 "For He shall give his angels charge over thee, to keep thee in all thy ways." — Psalm 91:11

The Partnership of Alignment

Throughout this book, we've explored thought, language, emotion, boundaries, rituals, and forgiveness. All are essential. They raise your frequency. They stabilize your new identity.

But here's the truth plainly: alignment is not mechanics alone. It is a relationship.
You are not alone in the field. You are co-creating with Infinite Intelligence. Your prayers, meditations, and gratitude rituals are not one-way broadcasts. They are conversations. The field has always been whispering back.

And when you surrender your need to control how blessings arrive, you open the gate for miracles.

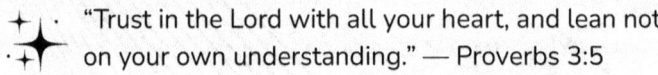 "Trust in the Lord with all your heart, and lean not on your own understanding." — Proverbs 3:5

The Next Level: Expansion Without End

Here is the final truth I want you to leave with: you are not done. Reaching alignment, establishing your new identity, raising your frequency—these are not endpoints. They are thresholds.

The universe itself is expanding. Stars are being born as you read this. Galaxies stretch further every second. And so must you.

Desire is not greed—it is divine order. You are called to want more, to grow more, to become more. Abraham Hicks says it best:

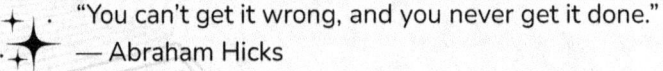 "You can't get it wrong, and you never get it done." — Abraham Hicks

Your new identity is not your final version. It is simply your current one. The higher version is already calling, already waiting. And God-consciousness is always inviting you forward.

Key Takeaways

○ The field is intelligent. Within it resides God-consciousness— the higher intelligence that pervades all life.

○ Spirit guides and angels walk with you, helping align your steps in unseen ways.

- ○ Alignment is not mechanics alone—it is a relationship with Infinite Intelligence.

- ○ Growth is eternal. Expansion is a divine order.

- ○ Gratitude and recognition of God-consciousness amplify your frequency and open the gate for miracles.

Afterword

Final Reflection

Pause. Breathe. Ask yourself:

- Can I sense the presence of something greater in the field around me?
- Have I lived moments that could only be explained by grace?
- How can I honor that intelligence daily—not just with rituals, but with recognition?
- What would it mean to live not only in alignment with my new self, but in partnership with God-consciousness?

Sit with these questions. They are not to be rushed. Because this is not the end. It is the beginning of a greater becoming.

> "You don't just attract what you want. You attract what you are — and you are more than matter, more than thought, more than body. You are a divine broadcast of Infinite Intelligence." — D. Knox

Closing Affirmation

Take a breath. Place your hand over your heart. Read these words slowly, as if each one is becoming your vibration:

"I release the weight of my past.

I honor the lessons, but I no longer carry the pain.

I choose alignment with my highest self.

I walk in the frequency of love, courage, and gratitude.

I recognize the Infinite Intelligence that moves through me.

I give thanks for the guidance of Spirit, angels, and the God-consciousness within the field.

I trust the rhythm of my becoming.

I am worthy of miracles.

I am worthy of expansion.

I am worthy of joy.

Today I declare:

I am aligned.

I am whole.

I am free.

"And the universe responds to what I AM." — D. Knox

Epilogue

A Letter to You

If you're here, pause. breathe. Take this in: you are not the same person who opened this book.

Life has a way of looping us in pain. But through this journey, you've broken cycles, lifted your frequency, and embodied a new identity.

This is not a theory. This is not a patch. This is a permanent recalibration of mind, body, and spirit.

I know this path works because I've lived it. I carried pain, addiction, and collapse — and

I rebuilt with alignment, coherence, and God-consciousness. What you hold is not just my story, but a framework to carry you into yours.

And now, the future opens before you.

A Vision Forward

Imagine a world where millions of people live aligned.

Where homes radiate peace instead of chaos.

Where families are raised in emotional coherence, not inherited loops.

Where leaders broadcast clarity, not fear.

Where communities embody love as frequency, not just as a word.

This is not a dream — it is a possibility. And it begins with one aligned person at a time. With you.

"As each of us raises our frequency, humanity itself rises."
— D. Knox

About the Author

David Knox was forged in generational fire—trauma, addiction, and dysfunction etched across both sides of his family. He endured the collapse of business and marriage, the strain of family breakdown, the trials of fatherhood, and the crucible of entrepreneurship—all of which became the ground of his transformation.

For more than two decades, David has sought truth beyond boundaries. Raised in Christianity, he expanded his studies to include Buddhism, Islam, and universal law, later drawing insights from modern teachers such as Abraham Hicks, Deepak Chopra, Dr. Joe Dispenza, and A Course in Miracles. Most recently, he immersed himself in quantum physics—consciousness, resonance, and coherence—where science confirmed what spirit had always revealed: thought shapes reality, and frequency creates form.

An entrepreneur across retail, hospitality, and real estate, David has long chosen the unconventional path. Now, he brings that same pioneering spirit to his life's true calling. The result is Quantum Identity Alignment—a revolutionary program, that fully integrate people into there higher self. Unlike traditional self-help, which requires piecing together dozens of books for incremental gains, this framework unifies the disciplines of spirituality, science, and lived practice into one powerful system. It delivers a permanent foundation for transformation by understanding frequency and true alignment— mind, body, and spirit into lasting coherence—so that readers don't just change for a moment, but ascend into their highest selves permanently.

"A revolutionary fusion of wisdom and science, created for a world rising into higher consciousness." — D. Knox

Resources & Next Steps

Extending the Ripple

Transformation is never meant to end with one person—it's a ripple that spreads outward, shaping families, communities, and even the collective field of consciousness. If this book has stirred something within you, I invite you to take the next steps and join the growing Quantum Identity Alignment community.

At www.quantumidal.com, you'll find resources to deepen your journey:

- o   Coaching Services – One-on-one and group coaching designed to help you embody alignment in every area of life.

- o   Workshops & Programs – Live and online workshops that explore the practices outlined in this book in greater depth.

- o   Digital Resources – Download the eBook, listen to the audiobook, and access additional tools for ongoing growth and development.

- o   Community Connection – Become part of the Quantum Identity Alignment community—a global network of seekers committed to raising frequency and living from higher consciousness.

Stay connected with me and our community through our social

platforms, where I share teachings, practices, and inspiration each week:

YouTube, TikTok, Facebook, and Instagram: @Quantumidal

This work is not a moment—it is a movement. By stepping into alignment, you not only transform your own life, you also extend the ripple to everyone around you. Let's rise together.

www.ingramcontent.com/pod-product-compliance
Lightning Source LLC
Chambersburg PA
CBHW070933130626
46555CB00001B/413